Cambridge Elements

Elements in Shakespeare and Pedagogy
edited by
Liam E. Semler
The University of Sydney
Gillian Woods
University of Oxford

TEACHING SHAKESPEARE'S THEATRE OF THE WORLD

Kristen Abbott Bennett
Framingham State University

Shaftesbury Road, Cambridge CB2 8EA, United Kingdom

One Liberty Plaza, 20th Floor, New York, NY 10006, USA

477 Williamstown Road, Port Melbourne, VIC 3207, Australia

314–321, 3rd Floor, Plot 3, Splendor Forum, Jasola District Centre, New Delhi – 110025, India

103 Penang Road, #05–06/07, Visioncrest Commercial, Singapore 238467

Cambridge University Press is part of Cambridge University Press & Assessment, a department of the University of Cambridge.

We share the University's mission to contribute to society through the pursuit of education, learning and research at the highest international levels of excellence.

www.cambridge.org
Information on this title: www.cambridge.org/9781009111096

DOI: 10.1017/9781009109888

© Kristen Abbott Bennett 2025

This publication is in copyright. Subject to statutory exception and to the provisions of relevant collective licensing agreements, no reproduction of any part may take place without the written permission of Cambridge University Press & Assessment.

When citing this work, please include a reference to the DOI 10.1017/9781009109888

First published 2025

A catalogue record for this publication is available from the British Library

ISBN 978-1-009-11109-6 Paperback
ISSN 2632-816X (online)
ISSN 2632-8151 (print)

Additional resources for this publication at www.cambridge.org/Bennett.

Cambridge University Press & Assessment has no responsibility for the persistence or accuracy of URLs for external or third-party internet websites referred to in this publication and does not guarantee that any content on such websites is, or will remain, accurate or appropriate.

For EU product safety concerns, contact us at Calle de José Abascal, 56, 1°, 28003 Madrid, Spain, or email eugpsr@cambridge.org

Teaching Shakespeare's Theatre of the World

Elements in Shakespeare and Pedagogy

DOI: 10.1017/9781009109888
First published online: November 2025

Kristen Abbott Bennett
Framingham State University

Author for correspondence: Kristen Abbott Bennett, kbennett5@framingham.edu

ABSTRACT: This Element engages with one of Shakespeare's greatest thought-experiments: *How does one navigate the 'theatre of the world'?* It invites students to examine how Shakespeare challenges this metaphor's vertical hierarchies in response to shifting understandings of cosmological order. Teachers will find rich contextual frameworks for exploring how Shakespeare envisions 'worlds' as emerging from dynamic variables, raising urgent questions about how identity and justice are environmentally constructed. Focal plays include *A Midsummer Night's Dream, As You Like It, Hamlet, Henry V, The Merchant of Venice*, and *Othello*. Each discussion features student-centred 'Explorations'. These play-specific classroom activities can also be adapted across Shakespeare's corpus and tailored for both secondary and university-level students. These exercises encourage non-linear critical and creative thinking, inviting students to contemplate big ideas and generate new perspectives about the shared points of contact between Shakespeare's world and their own.

KEYWORDS: Shakespeare pedagogy, Critical and creative thinking, Teaching perspective, Student-centred instruction, Constructing identities and justice, Shakespeare

© Kristen Abbott Bennett 2025

ISBNs: 9781009111096 (PB), 9781009109888 (OC)
ISSNs: 2632-816X (online), 2632-8151 (print)

Contents

	Prologue: Enter Chorus	1
1	The Theatre of the World in Ancient, Mediaeval, and Early Modern Contexts	5
2	Thematic Explorations of the Theatre of the World	21
3	Formal Explorations of the Theatre of the World	53
	Coda: Who's There?	90
	References	93

Prologue: Enter Chorus

The approaches to teaching Shakespeare here engage his greatest thought-experiment: How does one navigate the 'theatre of the world' (*theatrum mundi*)? In Shakespeare's day, this metaphor conveyed a complex mode of thinking about one's place on earth, in the cosmos and in the afterlife. When the Globe Theatre was erected in 1599, it reportedly boasted the motto *totus mundus agit histrionem*, or 'all the world's a stage', and architecturally figured the metaphor: the boards the mundane world, the actors humanity and the audience, in seats that rise up to the sky, the celestial audience judging the performance. Over time, this well-worn expression has been reduced to a cliché. But as I'll discuss in Section 1, Shakespeare's plays recognise the theatre of the world as a dynamic framework that challenges singular perspectives and elicits complex thinking.

This Element aspires to help teachers raise questions about big ideas and complex problems in their classrooms. What constitutes a 'world'? How do perception and reality contribute to worldmaking? How might worlds be informed by the 'theatres' that contain them? The focus here is not on 'theatre' as a literal performance space. From the perspective of the metaphor, the 'theatre' is capacious, conveying the socio-political, environmental and cosmological contexts from which 'worlds' emerge. In the classroom, this figure invites today's students to think about constructions of identity and justice over time and at scale.

Section 1 provides an overview of the theatre of the world's early history and examines how Shakespeare challenges its vertical hierarchies in response to changing understandings of cosmological order. With a basic contextual framework for thinking with the theatre of the world, teachers can encourage their students to ask, alongside Shakespeare, what happens to a metaphor when the science underpinning it dissolves?[1] Section 2 examines how Shakespeare thematically develops the metaphor in *As You Like It*, *The Merchant of Venice* and *Othello*. Here, one is invited to join Shakespeare as he puzzles through the shifting senses of

---

[1] Suparna Roychoudhury also raises this question in the context of science and the imagination (2018: 22).

perception, justice and worldliness – both on earth and beyond – that inform both 'theatre' and 'world'. Section 3 explores how *A Midsummer Night's Dream*, *Henry V* and *Hamlet* formally enact thought-experiments that put pressure on this device's elemental components by way of interacting literary devices, not limited to the play-within-a-play. Play summaries are not included as they are plentifully available elsewhere. I have chosen these plays primarily because they are frequently taught in schools, excepting perhaps *As You Like It*. Yet as I demonstrate, this play's famous 'Seven Ages of Man' set-piece is one of Shakespeare's most powerful explorations of the metaphor's shifting cosmology. The division of 'thematic' and 'formal' approaches is somewhat artificial; one facet of Shakespeare's brilliance is how he combines theme and form to create powerful effects. But instructors hopefully will find these designations useful starting points for classroom discussions and activities.

Each subsection provides historical and critical context to help teachers frame in-class conversations that are both play-specific and broadly applicable throughout Shakespeare's corpus. These discussions frame the *theatrum mundi* as a rhetorical device that raises questions about how early modern approaches to understanding the world – through humoural theories, racial and geographical difference, environmental phenomena, astronomy and cosmology – have ongoing repercussions in contemporary debates surrounding identity and socio-political constructions of judicial equity for planetary inhabitants today. Highlighted throughout is how this metaphor carries a cognitive imperative to simultaneously consider two perspectives and generate new ones. At stake for Shakespeare and ourselves is how we make knowledge in a world when 'order' is hard to come by. Throughout, 'Explorations' provide pedagogies that are grounded in practising non-linear critical and creative thinking, in challenging historical and personal biases and helping students recognise shared points of contact between Shakespeare's world and theirs.

Twenty-first-century global citizens share much with those at the turn of the seventeenth century: disruptive weather patterns, deadly epidemics and an information revolution that has contributed to nationalistic and racial prejudices, anti-environmentalism and censorship. Positioning events at the turn of the seventeenth century as analogous to those in the twenty-first may not be historically 'correct', but can help students recognize their connections to different points in time and space.

These approaches are designed to help students develop what Thomas P. Mackey and Trudi E. Jacobson call 'metaliteracies'. Metaliteracies describe a network of cognitive, affective, behavioural and metacognitive (self-reflective) learning outcomes (2011: 70). Mackey and Jacobson contend that 'metaliteracy prepares individuals to be thoughtful and collaborative producers of information in all forms including text, image, sound, and multimedia' (2011: 2). Metaliterate learners are not merely consumers of information but *producers* of knowledge. Attaining metaliteracies is an active process by which one recursively tests and adapts one's belief systems as they accommodate new information. Mackey and Jacobson developed these frameworks in direct response to the 'post-truth' information landscape one finds throughout the globe today. The *Oxford English Dictionary* named 'post-truth' the word of the year in 2016, but it also reflects the conditions under which Shakespeare was writing at the turn of the seventeenth century.

Like Shakespeare, we live in a time when personal belief systems tend to override facts. The *OED* defines 'post-truth' as 'Relating to or denoting circumstances in which objective facts are less influential in shaping political debate or public opinion than appeals to emotion and personal belief' (adj. 2). Steve Tesich popularises the term in an article that discusses how twentieth-century televised politics in the United States (e.g. the atrocities of the Vietnam War, the Watergate scandal and the Iran Contra affair) gave rise to the supremacy of nationalistic hubris at the expense of truth (1992). Following these events, '[Americans] came to equate truth with bad news and we didn't want bad news anymore, no matter how true or vital to our health as a nation. We looked to our government to protect us from the truth' (1992: np). Tesich's bleak conclusions now seem painfully prescient: 'We [Americans] are rapidly becoming prototypes of a people that totalitarian monsters could only drool about in their dreams. All the dictators up to now have had to work hard at suppressing the truth. We, by our actions, are saying that this is no longer necessary' (1992: np). The fallout from these attitudes has had dire consequences for educational systems and information literacy worldwide.

Post-truth information-cultures compound the challenges of what Liam E. Semler pejoratively – and rightly so – calls 'SysEd'. According to Semler, SysEd describes neoliberal, professionalised education models that position 'educators and students in an interlocking network of systems that deliver standardisation, measurement and compliance' (2016: 3). These approaches employ data-driven assessment models to project student 'success' in terms of college admissions, subsequent starting salaries and future earnings. But SysEd-inspired curricula fail to prioritise the intellectual flexibility that rapidly changing workplaces demand. To that end, the suggested teaching strategies throughout this Element are deliberately expansive. Activities are not designed to guide students toward concrete 'answers' but instead to help them practice habits of mind whereby they learn to ask questions and, by using textual evidence, to generate, test and support hypotheses. My aim is to support instructors as they situate students to discover their own best practices for critical and creative thinking, empowering them in the classroom and beyond.

Once students are introduced to the diverse perspectives carried in the theatre of the world metaphor, they can recognise their roles and contributions to the larger systems that comprise their world stages. Equally important, they learn to recognize that their 'world' is someone else's 'theatre' and vice versa. Shakespeare's dramatisations of the *theatrum mundi* generate multiple perspectives from which students can apprehend how dominant culture power structures are reified through laws, institutional practices and language. But language, especially the figurative language of poets and dramatists, *also* provides a vehicle for questioning these structures and systems, for challenging them to be more equitable and compassionate. The discussions and activities I share here are designed to help students identify how such questions emerge across Shakespeare's works. By encouraging students to develop habits of mind that consider all possibilities (CAP), I hope they will generate critical whole-person perspectives from which they can navigate whole-world turmoil.

1 The Theatre of the World in Ancient, Mediaeval, and Early Modern Contexts

The *theatrum mundi* has circulated for millennia, but Shakespeare's 'Seven Ages of Man' speech in *As You Like It* has become its touchstone: 'All the world's a stage, / And all the men and women merely players. / They have their exits and their entrances, / And one man in his time plays many parts' (Shakespeare, 2024b: 2.7.146–147). This section introduces the *theatrum mundi* from three intersecting perspectives. The first part surveys the evolution of the metaphor from its ancient origins to early modernity. Initially, it invited one to contemplate one's actions with an eye toward a perfect justice that would be adjudicated in the afterlife. Over time, it accrues complexity in response to changing worldviews and understandings of the cosmos. The second part situates the theatre of the world in sixteenth-century cosmographical contexts. Tellingly, this metaphor enjoys a renaissance of popularity concurrent with scientific discoveries that 'unsphered' the heavens, changing understandings of the cosmos and disrupting already unstable conceptions of world 'order'. In closing, I invite readers to take a virtual field trip to outer space in this section's complementary film: *This Universal Theatre*. This short film vivifies the *topos* in both its historical and contemporary contexts (Video 1). 'Explorations' invite students to engage with changing approaches to worldmaking across space and time.

The theatre of the world's associations with morality and the divine adjudication of post-mortem reward or punishment may seem old-fashioned from today's secular perspectives. Tiffany Stern wittily conceptualises a 'heaven-earth-hell sandwich' (2013: 18) that John Gillies claims 'is always morally inflected. Its usual sense is that human life is as vain and empty as a comedy' (2016: 60). Both Stern and Gillies emphasise a moralising imperative that carries a tacit threat: behave on earth, or else. As I will demonstrate, however, Shakespeare's thematic and formal manipulations of this theatrical metaphor engage a sceptical view of cosmographical contemplation, raising questions about received wisdom, hierarchies of justice as well as what constitutes a 'world'.

Comparisons between humans and actors have circulated for thousands of years. Plato draws a simile between humans and puppets, 'put

Figure 1 *Theatre of the World*. Illustration by Lee Smiley Designs.

together either for [the gods'] play or for some serious purpose' (*Laws* I.644d). Later, Petronius figures Plato's 'puppets' as actors in his satire, *The Satyricon*:

> The strollers act their farces upon the stage, each one his part, The father, son, the rich man, all are here, But soon the page is turned upon the comic actor's art, The masque is dropped, the make-ups disappear! (1922: 80)

Petronius mocks 'the strollers' on the world stage as they perform their 'farces'. These performances are 'farcical' because the players take their worldly identities seriously. When the 'page turns' and they leave this world for the next, the actors will be judged not by their 'masques' of seeming, but according to their true selves. As a genre, satire sends up human inclinations toward hubris, as well as darker flaws. Satire tempers the ironies and hypocrisies of human behaviour with humour to keep an audience's attention while delivering its critique. As the theatre of the world circulates through the ages, its satirical targets extend from individuals to political states.

John of Salisbury's twelfth-century treatment of Cicero's 'Dream of Scipio' in *The Policraticus: On the Frivolities of Courtiers and the Footprints of*

Philosophers extends the *theatrum mundi's* horizons from the individual to the state and from the earth to the cosmos. Cicero's 'Dream' was first published in *The Republic* and posits cosmographical contemplation as a path to political virtue. Cicero's text does not invoke the theatrical metaphor directly, but the ideas of performance and judgment associated with the *topos* resonate throughout. As Cicero situates Africanus and Scipio at the edges of the earth's atmosphere, they have a view much like that in the famous photo 'Earthrise' (2000: VI.13–17) (Figure 2).

Africanus and Scipio remain in the so-called sublunary world, but from there they can apprehend the spheres above and the earth below. This journey is an exercise in perspective. Africanus advises Scipio: 'If you will only look on high and contemplate this eternal home and resting place, you will no longer attend to the gossip of the vulgar herd or put your trust in human reward ... Virtue ... should lead you on to true glory' (2000: VI.22). By looking 'up' and contemplating the vastity of the universe, the music of the spheres and the promise of everlasting joy, one may be inspired to pursue

Figure 2 *Earthrise–Apollo 8*, Justin Cowart, Wikimedia

a virtuous life. Cicero's work is grounded in the premise that if the citizens of a state are honourable, their integrity will extend to the republic at large.

The other side of this cosmographical coin emphasises the Petronian 'farce' of worldly ambition. Scipio observes how 'the starry spheres were much larger than the earth ... the earth seemed to me so small that I was scornful of our empire, which covers only a single point ... upon its surface' (2000: 6.15). The Stoic philosopher Seneca later augments Cicero's observation, exclaiming: 'Is this the pinpoint which is divided by sword and fire by many nations? How ridiculous are the boundaries of mortals!' (1999: I Pref 8). Or, as Shakespeare's Puck will say: 'Lord! What fools these mortals be' (2024a: 3.2.117). Here, the 'boundaries of mortals' are ridiculous because they are artificial human constructions and bear no weight in relation to the cosmos. We mortals are 'fools' because we take life on earth too seriously.

John recasts the *theatrum mundi* into Christian cosmological contexts. For John, life is a 'comedy' because the actors get swept up in their own performances despite being under the direction of Lady Fortune: 'The individuals become subordinate to the acts as the play of mocking fortune unfolds itself in them' (1972: 172). Echoing Cicero and Seneca, John closes with a reflection on the contrast between mortal decay on planet earth that contrasts the fixed heavens above that crown the 'sun of justice' (1972: 176–177). In John's Ptolemaic universe, the earth is at the centre of the universe; the 'sun' of justice homonymically invokes the 'son' of God, Jesus Christ. Like Cicero, John reminds readers that virtue is its own reward; it leads to a good life and a healthy political state. If that fails to persuade, then readers are reminded that life on earth may not be fair, but perfect justice awaits in the afterlife – for better or for worse. One's performance on the world's stage will be judged by God, and rewarded or punished according to a vertical logic whereby the good go 'up' to heaven and the bad go 'down'. John's incorporation of cosmographical contemplation with the theatrical metaphor expands the *theatrum mundi's* capacity, rendering it ideal for apprehending increasingly dynamic structures of world order. Yet, over time, one finds that this system is a complex one, with many layers of adjudication on earth and in the heavens.

Later, in the fourteenth-century, Geoffrey Chaucer's *The Parliament of Fowls* tests the premises on offer from John and Cicero as the speaker narrates his reading of Macrobius' *Commentary* on Cicero's *Dream*. Here, Chaucer's speaker nods off while reading about Cicero's Scipio and dreams of a government run by birds. This poem starts off looking to the cosmos, but then turns to contemplate what constitutes natural order and knowledge-making on earth. The birds have gathered to judge which male should be awarded a female eagle's love. Their arguments are raucous and ridiculous, perhaps not unlike the lawmakers Chaucer may be parodying. Ultimately, they fail to reach agreement, and the dreamer experiences no revelation upon awakening. Overall, the poem mocks individual, political and scholarly pretensions to ego, power and knowledge. As Susan Crane observes, Chaucer's riff on Cicero's Scipio translates the driving question of 'How do I save myself?' to *simultaneously* ask 'What's happening here [on earth]?' (2017: 3).

Chaucer's two-fold interpretation of the cosmological metaphor similarly resonates throughout Erasmus' *The Praise of Folly*, a sixteenth-century work that Shakespeare draws upon frequently. Like John's *Policraticus* and Chaucer's *Parliament*, Erasmus' *Folly* contemplates the relations between divine and mundane justice. Here, Folly – a woman – tempers the 'perverse prudence' that dominates moralising interpretations of the *theatrum mundi* and chastises those who 'insist that the play should not be *a play*' (1979: 44; my emphasis). Folly further contends: 'Now the whole life of mortal men, what is it but a sort of play, in which various persons make their entrances in various costumes, and each one plays his own part until the director gives him his cue to leave the stage?' (1979: 43–44).[2] Like Chaucer's *Parliament*, Erasmus' romp through the idiosyncrasies of the human 'comedy' recognises the pluralities of moral justice in both mundane and divine contexts.[3]

---

[2] Shakespeare's Jacques will augment Folly's four ages of man and offer seven, a departure I'll discuss in more detail in Section 2 (1979: 20).

[3] Erasmus amplifies the theatre of the world's reliance upon perspective when he alludes to Plato's 'Allegory of the Cave' (1979: 43, 72–73). This short work can help students think about perspective and what constitutes 'enlightenment' at various scales of relation. Open access editions are easily found online.

By the end of the sixteenth century, the *theatrum mundi's* internal dialectic had developed both to contemplate and challenge received wisdom, especially in the context of judicial systems. Although Gillies contends Shakespeare's take is 'invariably' pessimistic, his discussion belies that observation. As Gillies traces this figure through Shakespeare's works, its employment in cartography, in humanist discourse, in the context of the Reformation and insofar as it reflects the tensions between reason and passion in philosophical discourses, he highlights the variegated positions that can emerge from thinking *with* the theatre of the world. Gillies' conclusion recognises this device as 'prophetically modern[;] ... the stress is more on the mutually reflective character of the theatre of the world and the life world and not at all on the supposed superiority of one over the other' (2016: 64). The *mise en abyme*, the play-within-a-play, enacts 'the infinite regress of the two mirrors [that have] the effect of both multiplying and dissolving: there are two theatres and/or two audiences, depending on which way one wants to look at it' (Gillies, 2016: 64). To say that this metaphor is unilaterally pessimistic, or that it articulates a single conceptual position during the sixteenth century, is unduly reductive.

The theatre of the world's rhetorical complexity can make it a moving target. I suggest approaching the metaphor as a cognitive frame that supports thinking with multiple points of view. Ayanna Thompson and Laura Turchi describe 'frame' in pedagogical contexts as 'a delimited, intentional and focussed approach to the multiplicity of interpretive lenses available' (2016: 23). The *theatrum mundi* presents us with two interpretive lenses: 'theatre' and 'world'. One can think of 'worlds' as microcosms that emerge from interactions with their surrounding 'theatres', or macrocosms. From this framework, students can practise attending to the details that articulate diverse perspectives, whether human or non-human, or that arise from different points in time, space and place. At the same time, this metaphor's complexity invites them to consider how conceptions of morality and justice may change depending upon the conditions that inform one's point of view.

Unfortunately, thanks to 'SysEd', many students have been conditioned to take a goal-oriented approach toward language (Semler, 2016). They want to figure out what a metaphor 'means' so they can do well on a test or move along as they read. Although Vandana Singh reminds us that 'a metaphor connotes something that exists in the abstract realm of the mind, hovering over and separated from physical reality', many standardised assessments, especially examinations, establish bilateral substitution paths that undercut abstract thinking (2024: 202). When contemplating 'to be, or not to be', students are directed towards an 'Ay, there's the point' (Shakespeare, *Ham.*, [1603] 2006: 7.115) style of thinking rather than sitting with: 'That is the question' (*Ham.*, [1623] 2006: 3.1.57).[4] Such end-directed, binary approaches to metaphor can make reading a chore, imperilling the joy one finds from puzzling into possibilities, from discovering meaningful analogues and from embracing the very ambiguity that Marc de Mey contends 'underlies aesthetic pleasure' (2006: 278). Institutional reliance on standardised forms of assessment may fail to take 'pleasure' into account for student learning. But teaching students to delight in the difficult, to adventure into the unknown, to posit and to test hypotheses surrounding linguistic possibility can help them navigate both the words and the worlds they live in.

Embracing metaphorical ambiguity also invites complex thinking about the critical work figurative language can do in the classroom. One objective is, as Huw Griffiths has argued, 'to move students away from reading the metaphor as a kind of crossword clue, the solution to which discerns what the phrase "really means". The aim is to replace this approach with a more playful attitude that is attentive ... [to] the words and phrases that are actually written and said' (2021: 7–8). Following Griffiths, one might ask students: What does a word literally convey in the context of a line/sentence? Then, as Adhaar Noor Desai suggests, we can invite them to 'riff' off the word and generate additional associations (2019: 28). Ruth Morse further reminds us that 'words are not always stable ... [and] ideas we test and disregard can be as important in our experience as those we retain' (2019: 95). Once students generate and test an array of possible associations, they can develop hypotheses about the interplay of sense and word.

By examining linguistic instability, students see how words and worlds are co-constructed, a process that mirrors early modern worldmaking theories

---

[4] Most theories of metaphor set up a binary path to interpretation, whether through the 'vehicle' and 'tenor' of I.A. Richards, or the 'principal' and 'subsidiary' connotations Max Black sets out, or even the 'primary' and 'secondary' terms of metaphor that Dennis Sobolev proposes as a way to recognise complexity (2008: 911).

and their analogues in cognitive theory, specifically those of 'parallel thinking'. Much as Jane Hwang Degenhardt and Henry S. Turner have argued that 'worlds can always be otherwise: they depend on a horizon of potentiality through which they are constantly being remade through our stories and our mutual recognition' (2021: 162), cognitive theorists contend 'parallel thinking emphasises allowing different ways of thinking to co-exist (rather than compete and cancel each other out), so that they can lead to solutions beyond the limits set by the problem rather than rushing to judgement. It is productive as opposed to reductive and aims to enrich and increase the complexity of a situation' (Moseley et al., 2005: 135). Parallel thinking is not linear, but instead encourages divergence by yoking more than one line of inquiry to another and eliciting creative approaches to complex problems.

Edward de Bono proposes parallel thinking as an 'antidote' to transactional, vertical models of knowledge-making. This model, known as CoRT (Cognitive Research Trust), encourages one to suspend instant judgement and attend to the multidimensionality of a given situation. This method's overarching ambition to consider all possibilitie and to subvert end-stopped thinking is a common thread throughout this Element's suggested activities (Moseley et al., 2005: 133–134).

EXPLORATION: WHAT CONSTITUTES A 'WORLD'?

Roland Greene recognises the word 'world' as a 'semantic engine' (2020: 149) that 'reflects changes in a network of related ideas [and] also changes those ideas by occasioning rethinking' (2020: 158). What might it mean that Shakespeare uses roughly six hundred and fifty-six variants of the word 'world' throughout his works (Open Source Shakespeare, 2023)?[5] In the following activity, students progressively identify the elements that constitute a 'world' from several perspectives.

---

[5] Counts will vary across editions. For full corpus searches, however, Open Source Shakespeare is suitable for both beginning and advanced students.

EXPLORATION (cont.)

Getting Started

1. Invite students to brainstorm a list of everything they associate with the 'world'.
2. Ask them to review their list and consider how they consider the 'world' as a simile: what is a world 'like'? Then they can consider how a 'world' emerges as a more capacious metaphor. For example, Shakespeare's 'all the world's a stage' initially sets forth a simile: the world is *like* a stage (2024b: 2.7.146). When one considers *how* the world is like a stage, it begins to emerge as a metaphor that stands in for the complexities of human life.
3. Ask students to consider how perspective contributes to the construction of 'worlds'. They can play with the following scenarios as they *construct* their hypothetical worlds:

   - What if you live on the moon?
   - What if you are an ant on a battlefield in ancient Rome?
   - What if your world were a literal stage?
   - Invite students to play with 'What if' constructions to generate their own scenarios.

4. Send students to Open Source Shakespeare or another concordance and invite them to study the 'world' in the context of Shakespeare's works. The sonnets and *As You Like It* offer especially ripe opportunities for exploration.

Question and Reflect

After students explore 'world' from different perspectives, ask: What criteria might determine a world-space? Are world boundaries natural or artificial? What might constitute a world from non-human perspectives? Teachers and students can discuss which associations were most interesting or surprising. If students fall back on generalisations like 'society', ask them to clarify how societies are constructed and who determines their structure.

> ### EXPLORATION (cont.)
>
> This activity aims to help students recognise 'worlds' as complex social, political, geographical, ecological and cosmographical systems. Here, students are positioned to experience learning outcomes across cognitive, metacognitive and behavioural domains. By reflecting upon world-making from diverse perspectives, students engage cognitively with their understandings of the 'world'. As they test, retest and reconsider situations and contexts from multiple viewpoints, they may enjoy behavioural outcomes in the form of new habits of mind. Exercising their conceptions of the 'world' from various viewpoints gives students an opportunity to realise how both words and worlds emerge from shared perspectives, from the 'mutual recognition' that Degenhardt and Turner have identified (2021: 162).

Shakespeare's plays juxtapose micro- and macrocosmic vantage points as he recasts the theatre of the world as a site for contemplating the profound complexities of world order, both on earth and in the heavens. Nearly all express scepticism about equity and worldmaking in the context of England's legislated shifts between Catholicism and what now is called Protestantism in 1533, 1547, 1553 and 1558, as well as the discovery of the so-called 'new world' and its indigenous peoples.[6] At the same time, advances in mathematics and astronomy challenged cosmological order. It may be no wonder that the *theatrum mundi* enjoys a burst of popularity that is exactly contemporary with events that changed people's understandings of both the terrestrial and cosmological domains.[7]

During Shakespeare's lifetime, the 'world' and the contexts from which it was generally understood changed radically. When Shakespeare was born

---

[6] I am using 'worldmaking' here in the sense of global imaginaries particular to early modern Western culture. See also Ramachandran (2015).

[7] The *theatrum mundi* prominently entered the scene of English print as these debates gained momentum. Barnaby Googe's popular 1565 translation of Marcellus Palingenio Stellato's *Zodiacke of Life* was republished in 1576 and 1588

in 1564, the location of earth itself was contentious. Until this time, Aristotle's (382–322 BCE) geocentric cosmology had dominated Western natural philosophy. Aristotle's model located earth at the centre of the universe 'under' the moon. This sublunar sphere contained astronomical and meteorological changeability, including the moon phases, comets, shooting stars, wind and lightning (Pumphrey, 2011: 36). 'Above' the moon, one was thought to find the heavenly spheres and fixed stars that held the promise of ultimate justice. Aristotle claimed these first seven spheres were solid containers carrying the planets through their orbits (then understood as Earth, the Sun, Mercury, Venus, Mars, Jupiter and Saturn). The eighth sphere comprised the fixed stars and was thought to be set into motion by a prime mover. Metaphorically, this outer realm represented a site of perfect justice that would be arbitrated in the afterlife.

On 11 November 1572, when Shakespeare was eight years old, a new star emerged in the constellation Cassiopeia. This star shined brightly day and night for two weeks, and remained visible in the night sky until March 1574 (Scovell, 2023). At first, astronomers thought it might be a weird comet. But its sustained appearance gave scholars time to develop advanced approaches to measuring parallax and to recognise that the supposedly 'fixed' stars were subject to volatility.[8] In astronomy, parallax describes the displacement of an object caused by an observer's shift in perspective; it is defined as the 'difference or change in the apparent position or direction of an object as seen from two different points' (*OED*, parallax, n.1). Anna Cetera-Włodarczyk, Jonathan Hope and Jaroslaw Włodarczyk have documented Shakespeare's sustained interest in how recent advances in measuring parallax had led to the dissolution of Aristotle's solid heavenly spheres and the

---

with additional marginal notes, including 'The world a stage play' (1588: 99). Following Googe, John Alday translated Pierre Boaistuau's French work, *Le Théâtre du Monde*; this text was reprinted in 1566, 1574, and 1581. Both Googe's and Alday's translations engage deeply with the *theatrum mundi* commonplace in the context of cosmographical contemplation.

[8] Mary Crane discusses how mathematical developments following this 1572 celestial event sparked changes in approaches to early modern knowledge making, leading to the confirmation of heliocentrism and the concept of infinity (2014: 21).

confirmation of Copernican heliocentrism (2021: 410). Shakespeare's connections with the Digges family, famous for their contributions to mathematics and astronomy, may also have sparked his imagination (Honan, 1999: 390–391, 405). Thomas Digges, along with fellow English astronomers Thomas Harriot and John Dee, supported Copernicus' theory and were at the forefront of recognising a new cosmological order.

Perhaps the most disruptive hypothesis that emerged following 1572 is Giordano Bruno's contention that astronomical infinity is truly infinite. Although Digges, Harriot and Dee recognised infinity, Hilary Gatti reminds us that they still 'conceived of this infinite space in static terms of a divine light' (Bruno and Gatti, 2018: xii). By contrast, Bruno's infinite infinity is not static but mutable. Bruno's ideas did not just threaten universal cosmologies, but also mundane ones. Gatti continues 'He knows that his infinite universe makes everything relative, destroying fixed centres and ideas by reducing earth and its inhabitants to a tiny speck within an overwhelmingly immense whole' (2018: xiii). Frances Yates has conjected a complex web of associations that link Shakespeare to Bruno's ideas, famously arguing that the mention of 'the school of night' in *Love's Labour's Lost* (Shakespeare, 2009: 4.3.246) references a circle of thinkers surrounding Sir Walter Raleigh who were engaged in these astronomical debates (1936: 89–101).[9] Although Yates takes scenes in this play as evidence that Shakespeare ridicules the new astronomy, that is not the case. Shakespeare does make fun of academic pedantry, of teachers who drone on about esoteric details. But he is not an intellectual reactionary and nor is there consistent evidence of his opposition to new cosmologies. Instead, as Tom Rutter rightly observes, Shakespeare's works illuminate 'the human dimension of these fields of inquiry: how people make sense of the things above them and how they use that understanding for their own purposes' (2024: 22). As I will discuss later in the context of *Hamlet*, Shakespeare's work reveals an insistent curiosity that interrogates what it means to be an actor in a theatrical multiplex that extends throughout the cosmos.

---

[9] I suggest George Peele may also link Shakespeare to Bruno's ideas given his documented familiarity in *The Honor of the Garter* (1593), a work published near the time Peele and Shakespeare likely collaborated on *Titus Andronicus*.

This section's companion film glosses these astronomical debates further, but for now, I should like to suggest that what Emma Smith has recognised as Shakespeare's essential 'gappiness' generates kaleidoscopic perspectives from which to engage with his plays. As Smith rightly observes, 'Sometimes Shakespeare's plays . . . propose adjacent worldviews that are fundamentally incompatible. These gaps are conceptual or ethical, and they open up space to think differently about the world and experience it from another point of view' (2021: 3). These shifting points of view are what – to my mind – make Shakespeare so exciting to teach. But they can be a challenge for students, especially when contemplating the *theatrum mundi* in its cosmographical contexts.

Shakespeare's works repeatedly suggest that he may have been thinking with parallax itself (Figure 3). Parallax's dependence upon two perspectives to ascertain a third term offers a frame for approaching the dual horizons of the 'theatre' of the 'world'. In the context of the *theatrum mundi's* astronomical associations, parallax can serve as a scalable thematic frame to help students think with and from multiple positions, however incompatible they may appear.

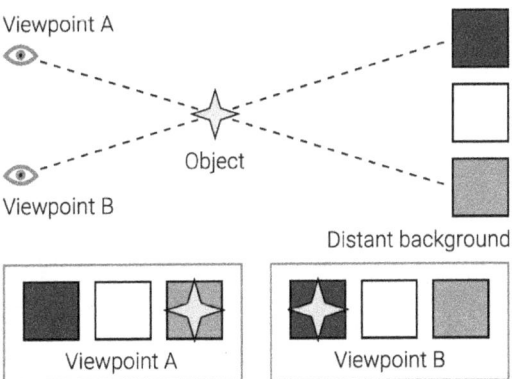

Figure 3 Parallax example. Justin Wick at English Wikipedia, CC BY-SA 3.0

In *A Midsummer Night's Dream* Theseus' poet models thinking with parallax; note the movement of the poet's eye:

> The poet's eye, in a fine frenzy rolling,
> Doth glance from heaven to Earth,
> from Earth to heaven,
> And as imagination bodies forth
> The forms of things unknown, the poet's pen
> Turns them to shapes and gives to airy nothing
> A local habitation and a name.
>
> (Shakespeare, 2024a: 5.1.12–18)

'Eye' and 'glance' roll down from heaven to Earth, and up from Earth to heaven. These optical perceptions combine to body forth a novel element: 'imagination'. Giving 'local habitation and a name' to 'airy nothing' analogises what complexity theorists call 'emergence'. As Claire Hansen explains, emergence 'is the process by which a system produces new phenomena through the interaction of its parts' (2017: 11). Thinking with parallax, with more than one viewpoint concurrently, can help students recognise such 'new phenomena' as they grapple with Shakespeare's gappiness and often contradictory images.

Theseus' speech is one of innumerable examples whereby Shakespeare employs the 'theatre' and the 'world' as separate inputs, as what cognitive theorists would call a double-scope integration model.[10] Here we see Shakespeare thinking *with* parallax and translating the mathematical formula into a figurative one. The translation of parallax from mathematics into metaphor is not new. When Thomas Digges shares his conclusion supporting Copernican heliocentrism resulting from advances in measuring parallax in his revisions of his father Leonard's *Prognostication*, he describes travelling on the 'wings and ladders of mathematics' and using his 'Geometricall Eyes' to apprehend distance in space (1576: Addition, Sig. N4 r). This distance informs the astronomer's perspective and his subsequent deductions. Inviting students to think with parallax gives them opportunities to recognise

---

[10] See Roberts for a discussion of conceptual blending and cognition (2018).

and question their own subjectivity. Additionally, by situating parallax as a reusable frame for generating hypotheses from several points of view, students have a real opportunity to think outside of the box – or if we want to get wild – to generate hypotheses that transcend geometry altogether.

As one might guess, the 'unsphering' of the heavens, the recognition of the universe as infinite and the circulating ideas about life on other planets upset conventional understandings of cosmographical order. But more importantly, for Shakespeare and his contemporaries, the essential analogue of the fixed heavens and perfect justice has been destroyed. Obviously, this cosmographical turmoil raises serious questions about the implications for justice on earth. But it also offers an opportunity to think about our shifting places in the world in relation to a changing cosmos, to think from the perspective of our planet, from the perspective of other worlds and from the perspectives of everything in between.

This Universal Theatre

Video 1 This Universal Theatre. Video file available at www.cambridge.org/Bennett.

This Universal Theatre positions students to radically re-imagine their perspectives, their respective 'worlds', today. This film first rehearses the cosmographical debates of Shakespeare's day that coalesce in the 1572 appearance of a 'new star' in Cassiopeia. It then takes viewers to the farthest reaches of the known universe before returning to Earth, asking them to contemplate the theatre of the world in the context of the multiplex of our expanding universe.

EXPLORATION: PERSPECTIVE AND PARALLAX

This Exploration invites students to reflect on their understandings of the 'world' before and after viewing *This Universal Theatre*.

Getting Started

Pre-viewing Freewrite

I suggest offering a Freewrite activity before showing the film so that students may collect their thoughts organically for a few minutes. Teachers might ask:

- How do you feel about your place in the world?
- What constitutes 'the world' to you at this moment?
- Is 'the world' limited to earth?
- Make a list of 'worlds' of different scales or sizes. Do they relate to one another? If so, how; if not, why not?

Question and Reflect

After viewing the film, ask students how their thinking about the foregoing questions may have changed. One may also discuss the following questions:

- How does one's perspective influence the way historical and current events are understood in relation to each other?
- How does thinking about and with parallax, that is to say from two different perspectives, change the way you think about your place in the world?
- How do facts about the universe relate to your understandings of perspective?
- Do things on macrocosmic scales – like distant galaxies – have any real bearing or impact on things at human scales? What about vice versa?

> EXPLORATION (cont.)
>
> - Do you think that human life might be a microcosm of the elements that make up the universe? If so, how? How does that impact your understanding of 'life'?
> - Are there differences between 'the world' and 'the universe'? How might these clarifications help students think with parallax in relation to the *theatre* of the *world*?
>
> Once students start grappling with these big ideas and generating hypotheses, they can reapply their questions and ideas to Shakespeare's plays and poetry. As they practise thinking from different perspectives at varying scales of relation, they may discover new insights about the subjectivity of worldmaking.

2 Thematic Explorations of the Theatre of the World

> All the world's a stage,
> and all the men and women merely players,
> they have their exits and their entrances,
> and one man in his time plays many parts,
> his acts being seven ages.
> (Shakespeare, 2024b: 2.7.146–150)[11]

The time has come to rescue Shakespeare's most well-known expression of the theatre of the world from cliché and to explore its complexity. What conditions would permit a person to 'exit' *before* they 'enter'? If a person plays many parts, are they doubling roles in a single play? How do perspective and local context intersect to establish multiple 'worlds'? This section examines Shakespeare's treatment of the variables comprising the

---

[11] Citations to *AYLI* hereafter follow Shakespeare, ed. B. Mowat, P. Werstine, M. Poston & R. Niles, 2024b, and will be given by act, scene and line.

theatrum mundi in the context of *As You Like It*, *The Merchant of Venice* and *Othello*. My aim is to help teachers and their students explore how shifting understandings of 'theatre' and 'world' impact micro- and macrocosmic constructions of identity, of socio-cultural and political hierarchies and of judicial equity.

'Much virtue in "if"': As You Like It

True to its title, *As You Like It* is a play that people tend to read as they like. Summaries typically highlight Rosalind and Orlando's romance and tease out questions surrounding role-play and gender. Indeed, Shakespeare's subversion of gender norms in *As You Like It* may reflect a broader questioning of 'order' itself, raising the question: Is there a natural order, or is change the touchstone of the world? Pamela Allen Brown and Jean E. Howard note that the best productions of the play invite the audience to suspend disbelief and explore 'what if' scenarios, a concept echoed in effective teaching methods. For example, Liam E. Semler advocates for classroom pedagogies driven by 'if' that he terms 'Ardenspaces' (see 2013: 53–79). 'Ardenspaces' disrupt traditional teacher-to-student knowledge transmission and encourage critical and creative thinking. Here, I suggest similar pedagogies of possibility that can help students develop habits of mind that exercise the 'virtue in "if"' (5.4.106–107). This subsection first examines the play's mirroring effects and Jacques' 'Seven Ages of Man' set-piece which reframes conventional cosmologies of 'worlds' and 'stages'. It then suggests strategies for incorporating scalable Collaborative Commonplace Book (CPB) assignments into lesson plans. Finally, it discusses how *As You Like It's* satirical elements target Elizabethan censorship.

Given this play's interest in the 'virtue of "if"' that extends through ninety-four repetitions of 'if', I should like to pose a question myself (my count; Shakespeare, 2024b). What if Shakespeare's multiplication of doubling throughout this play – two settings, two pairs of two brothers, Rosalind's two genders, two courtly romances, two pastoral romances and two satirists – extends beyond character development and comedy to engage the generative potential of arithmetic? Although mathematics is a discourse partially grounded in certainties like 2+2=4, it can also be positioned in the probable and the possible.

If the insistent doubling in *As You Like It* suggests a mathematical proposition, it may reflect Shakespeare's curiosity about what can be learned from then-recent advances in measuring planetary parallax. As discussed in Section 1, parallax involves calculating distance from two perspective points, and it serves as a metaphor for understanding how two viewpoints can combine to provide a more accurate understanding of a third term. To illustrate parallax, try this exercise: cover one eye and observe the view, then cover the other eye and notice how the field of vision shifts. This experiment can also be done with auditory stimuli by covering one ear and then the other. What initially appears as a clear pattern of doubling becomes more complex, revealing variegated positions that challenge linear interpretation.

This multiplicity is mirrored in Shakespeare's famous phrase, 'All the world's a stage', and the 'Seven Ages of Man' set-piece (2.7.146–173). While the Four Ages of Man has circulated for millennia, Shakespeare's departures from then-popular renderings, including Desiderius Erasmus' *The Praise of Folly*, and Barnabe Googe's translation of Palingenio's *Zodiacke of Life* are noteworthy.[12] Unlike Erasmus' standard four ages of infancy, youth, maturity and second childishness, or Palingenio's descriptive augmentation to five 'miseries of man from birth to the grave' (1588: 100), Shakespeare's seven ages appear unique, especially insofar as they correspond with the then-known seven planets of the solar system and conclude in dissolution:[13]

---

[12] The Four Ages of Man are connected to The Four Bodily Humours, The Four Directions and more; see Phillips (2023). Stuart Gillespie has identified Googe's translation of Palengenio's *Zodiacke*, specifically the chapter 'Virgo', as the source for 'All the world's a stage' both here and in the Globe Theatre's purported motto (2016). Shakespeare also appears to have been inspired by Palengenio's descriptive augmentations to infancy, childhood, youth, adulthood and old age (1588: 100–101).

[13] William H. Steffen (2023) cites John Anthony Burrow's 1988 work, *The Ages of Man*, that draws an analogue between the seven ages of man, the then-known

> All the world → Earth
> Infant → Sun
> Schoolboy → Mercury
> Lover → Venus
> Soldier → Mars
> Justice → Jupiter
> Pantaloon → Saturn
> Sans everything → Infinity (2.7.146–173)

From the perspective of sixteenth-century popular astrology, and the associations of planets with personal characteristics, one may see how each age of humanity corresponds to a cosmological element. This tacit analogy between life stages and orbiting planetary bodies recognises the plurality of 'worlds' a single person might encounter on their journey through time. It also conveys a pluralistic interpretation of the planets from both pagan and Christian perspectives. 'All the world' clearly signals Earth. The infant child parallels the sun by taking advantage of the homonym 'son'. The schoolboy is a novel addition to earlier models and can be associated with the Greek Mercury, who rules eloquence and communication. From here, the lover's association with Venus, the soldier's with Mars and the justice's with Jupiter follow directly. The 'slippered Pantaloon' suggests an Ovidian kind of Saturn, past his prime and overthrown by his children (Kline, *Metamorphoses* 2020: I.1–20). The final age, 'sans everything' is not necessarily nihilistic, or even bleak, but may signal the infinite possibilities that lie in the stars and space beyond Saturn, then the farthest planet yet identified in our solar system.[14]

'Worlds' emerge here as both material entities and as determined by time and experience. Jane Hwang Degenhardt and Henry S. Turner have discussed theories of regionalism as a way of thinking about early modern worldmaking; regions are 'not marginal to a centre nor are they central to

> seven planets, and the seven days of God's creation. But neither discusses how Jacques' formula departs from precedents to contemplate infinity.

[14] The total negation here suggests that Shakespeare is thinking with Giordano Bruno's infinite infinity (see Section 1, page tbd).

a margin: they are worlds unto themselves always connected to other places but remaining distinct from them' (2021: 161). But these regions and worlds are not limited to geographical spaces, or for that matter, terrestrial spaces: 'They are maintained through the circulation of people and objects . . . [of] stories of origin and belonging' (2021: 161). Worlds manifest as an element of personal selfhood, much as an individual's identity contributes to world-making through their interactions in mutually recognised spaces and communities. Shakespeare explores how worlds are made and remade through the characters' interactions in, across and through the worlds they encounter. If we think about what Semler calls the dynamic 'linguistic architecture' of if-clauses in *As You Like It*, we may see them as mirroring the changing architecture of the cosmos and begging questions about the possibilities that lie beyond singular conceptions of the 'world' (2013: 48).

EXPLORATION: COLLABORATIVE COMMONPLACING

Collaborative Commonplace Book (CPB) assignments invite teachers to encourage students to practise intellectual risk-taking with peers in low-stakes assignments. Students respond to open-ended prompts by crafting multimedia responses in which they collect, reflect and question their findings. Students work in shared GoogleSlide decks, each contributing a slide. In addition to quoting or 'snipping' text, making observations and posing questions, students are invited to think creatively with visual media. These prompts encourage associative, generative thinking (see Supplementary Material, Appendix 1). In this spirit, one might think of these CPB assignments as dissolving the 'spheres' of linear discussion and exploring spaces of infinite possibility.

The peer-to-peer engagement in these shared slide decks can stimulate strong learning communities regardless of class size or teaching modality. Using the shared CPBs as a starting point for class discussions and response essays fosters a critical and creative collaborative space that can lead to promising and exciting insights. The following sample prompts may be recombined to elicit 'what-if' thinking in the classroom.

EXPLORATION (cont.)

Getting Started

Pre-reading Prompt for Students

> Your aim is to brainstorm how you might describe 'the theatre of the world.' Visit the Folger Shakespeare Library's 'Theatre of the World' media group (https://digitalcollections.folger.edu/view/group/211754). This collection of images illustrates diverse perspectives surrounding the *theatrum mundi*. Look through the images and choose one that you find especially interesting. Paste it on your slide and make at least two observations about how it speaks to the 'theatre of the world' – you might start by thinking about the elements that make up a 'theatre' and the elements that make up a 'world.' Next, pose a question for class discussion.

This sample of student work emerged from an in-class exercise designed to introduce undergraduate students to the logistics of Commonplacing in GoogleSlides (Figure 4). Students had no prior knowledge about the 'theatre

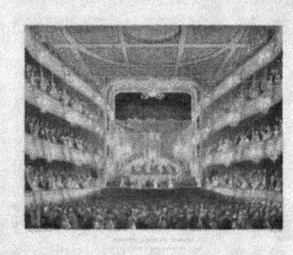

Figure 4 Sample Commonplace Book slide. Image reproduced with permission from Sabrina Grammatic, Sofia Wilson and Leighah Beausoleil.

EXPLORATION (cont.)

of the world'; it was the first day of class. We discussed how to capture screen images using 'snipping' tools, how to use Alt-text to make images accessible for screen readers and how to cite sources.[15] The unpredictability of students' contributions to the class CPBs has an added bonus: teachers learn new things as well. This group's focus on the relationships between the audience and the stage helped me introduce these roles in the context of the 'theatre of the world', and led to a lively discussion about the attentiveness of judicial powers to the 'performances' they adjudicate.

Additional CPB prompts are listed next. I suggest following each by asking students to generate a question for class discussion. Students may find this last step the most challenging as it requires them to think through the implications of their observations, to test their premises and to reflect upon their own and others' possible biases.

- Instruct students to select a quotation from the day's reading that sparks their interest, or speaks to a concept you want them to think with. What interests them? Ask them to illustrate their selection as they envision it with an image from the wild (i.e. the internet).
- Ask students to choose a quotation or screenshot from a supplementary reading or video that is loosely related to the day's assignment. *Shakespeare Reloaded's* 'Shakeserendipity' activities offer terrific models (2015). Teachers may also direct students to the Crash Course video series (Green and Green, 2012) and select related episodes.
- Instruct students to illustrate the concepts they're discussing with background images, memes, or other visualisations.
- Ask students to practise thinking with parallax and to generate observations about concepts that emerge from taking two perspectives into account.
- Ask students to illustrate how a line, scene or concept makes them feel using a meme, a .gif or a favourite song.

---

[15] See Copeland (2023) for help adding Alt-text in Google Slides.

> ### EXPLORATION (cont.)
>
> When generating a question for class discussion, less experienced students can benefit from recalling simple formulas like the journalist's trick: 'I want to know who/what/when/where/how/why'. Or, to encourage deeper critical thinking, Douglas Lanier's 'Definition questions', 'Comparison-contrast questions', 'Dramatic context questions' and 'Audience effect-questions' provide excellent guidance (2019: 140).
>
> ## Question and Reflect
>
> *Capstone Portfolio Assignment*: If one assigns regular CPBs, then a Capstone Portfolio Assignment with an accompanying metacognitive reflection encourages students to synthesise their learning of a unit or a course. For the portfolio, ask students to review the slides they generated throughout the term and to reorganise them into conceptual groups (e.g. time, gender or macrocosms). By outlining a rationale for their conceptual frame and reflecting on how their understanding of the course material changed over time, students reinforce their learning and realise a great sense of accomplishment.

Jacques' juxtaposition of this 'miserable world' (2.7.13) with his laughter 'sans intermission' marks him as a satirist who delights in calling people out on their bad behaviour, even if he is sometimes a hypocrite (2.7.33). He covets Touchstone's motley because it is the garb of the courtly licensed fool, and that licence gives permission to speak truth to power without repercussions. But in both the play and Shakespeare's England, speaking freely was not always an option.

As You Like It has been identified as Shakespeare's most topical play and one that engages directly with then-contemporary satire and literary politics. It was entered into the Stationer's Register on 4 August 1600, on the heels of the 1599 'Bishop's Ban' that prohibited the publication of several named satires, including works by some of Shakespeare's collaborators and all histories. As the list of prohibited literary genres proceeded, it grew so broad as to give censors the right to suppress nearly anything they liked.[16]

When the Bishops targeted printed satire, they didn't curtail its production, but redirected it into the theatres.[17] Celia's and Touchstone's exchange in the first act has one foot in fiction and another in Elizabethan London. In the play, Celia's father, Duke Frederick, has usurped his older brother's power, taken over the court and sent him into exile. Touchstone is Duke Senior's licensed fool, but Celia warns him that his 'licence' has expired under the new regime:

Celia:	Speak no more of him [Duke Frederick]; you'll be whipped for taxation one of these days.
Touchstone:	The more pity that fools may not speak wisely what wise men do foolishly.
Celia:	By my troth, thou sayest true; for since the little wit that fools have was silenced, the little foolery that wise men have makes a great show. (1.2.83–89)

When Celia warns Touchstone that he may be whipped for 'taxation', she describes the punishment he may incur if he speaks freely; here 'taxation' describes censure or reproof. Touchstone alludes to Erasmus' Folly when he laments the suppression of satire: 'fools may not speak wisely what wise men do foolishly' (1.2.85–86). But it is Celia's line, 'since the little wit that fools have was silenced, the little foolery wise men have makes a great show', that invokes London at the turn of the seventeenth century (1.2.87–88). As James Shapiro remarks, these lines provide a 'rare piece of editorialising the ban and its aftermath' (2006: 219).

---

[16] For discussions about the Bishop's Ban, see Richard A. McCabe (1981); Kristen Abbott Bennett (2022: 2–3).

[17] Although *As You Like It* was entered into the Stationer's Register on 4 August 1600, it may be telling that it was not published until 1623 (Shakespeare Documented, 2024).

Jacques paints a picture of this aftermath as he raises a question that is as pressing now as it was then:

> ... what is he of basest function
> That says his bravery is not on my cost,
> Thinking that I mean him, but therein suits
> His folly to the mettle of my speech?
> There then. How then, what then? Let me see wherein
> My tongue hath wronged him. If it do him right,
> Then he hath wronged himself. If he be free,
> Why then my taxing like a wild goose flies
> Unclaimed of any man. (2.7.72–90)

Jacques' overarching question here is: What kind of world is it when calling people out for bad behaviour has become worse than the behaviour itself? Today's students are likely familiar with this problem and may pause to consider the socio-political repercussions of state-mandated censorship. What shared points of contact emerge between the world of *As You Like It* and their own? How might insights generated from Shakespeare's play help one to navigate an emerging world 'order' that is characterised by political chaos?

As You Like It provides an opportunity to think about the 'theatre of the world' from near-infinite perspectives, including and importantly its origins in satire. Early renderings of the metaphor offered broad-stroke, Horatian-style satire that mirrored humanity's common hypocrisies while reminding them that ultimate judgement awaited. For Shakespeare and his contemporaries, however, the *theatrum mundi* evolved to query both divine and mundane judicial systems. Simultaneously, satire had progressed into a genre that was no longer easily categorised. It too was adapting to changes in world order, not least of which included institutional censorship. Although here and in *The Merchant of Venice*, Shakespeare openly engages the satirical elements of the *theatrum mundi*, as we shall see in *Othello*, his treatments following the ban are more oblique.

'Which is the Merchant, which is the Jew': The Merchant of Venice

As You Like It gives us Shakespeare's most famous articulation of the 'theatre of the world', but he had already been thinking with the metaphor when writing *The Merchant of Venice*. From one perspective, this play grapples directly with John of Salisbury's apposing descriptions of life in the *theatrum mundi* as a 'comedy' and as a 'trial' (1938: 171–172). For John, both life's comedy and its trials are rooted in humanity's bodily, earthly desires that controvert high-minded devotion to God and the afterlife. For Shakespeare, the relations between humanity and justice are not so clear-cut. This play raises questions about how the bodily 'humours' interact with the *theatrum mundi's* associations with justice, as well as what constitutes equity in a cosmos governed by mutability.

The first part of this subsection invites students to explore the capaciousness of 'comedy' and provides pre- and post-reading activities to help students examine this play's generic ambiguity. It then introduces early modern medical theories and explores the human body's relation to earth, to the cosmos and to justice in the *theatrum mundi*, notably through the lens of the three main characters: Antonio, Portia and Shylock. Although some instructors avoid teaching this play because of its upsetting anti-Semitic attitudes, I follow Paula Marantz Cohen and believe that it provides 'the very ingredients needed to defend against anti-Semitic thinking, though in a nuanced rather than a simplistic, finger-wagging way' (2021: 39). For example, Shylock's famous 'Hath not a Jew eyes' speech provides an ideal opportunity to help students mark the turns of language and logic that he uses to construct his identity in relation to the Venetian Christians (Shakespeare, 2006b: 3.1.48–60).[18] Attentive analysis of the play's Jewish and Christian characters will fail to exempt any from deep shortcomings. Ultimately, this section aims to help students generate perspectives from which to consider how identity and justice are constructed by the interactions between individuals from dominant and marginalised cultures.

---

[18] Citations to *MV* hereafter follow Shakespeare, ed. L. Marcus, 2006b, and will be given by act, scene and line.

The Merchant of Venice's generic designation of comedy is an uneasy one. This discomfort is partly because, as Lanier notes, 'comedy and humour are not the same thing' (2019: 144). Additionally, during Shakespeare's time, generic distinctions are markedly fluid, and better resemble the early modern humoral theories I discuss shortly than the clear-cut taxonomies that modernity retro-projects. Much as humoral fluids are impacted by interactions between an individual and their environment, genre can be informed by editors, performers and audiences as a play takes diverse forms over time. How do genre expectations inform one's experience of a play, or literary work? What consequences might follow?

EXPLORATION: GENRE

Getting Started

As a pre-reading exercise, I suggest inviting students to contemplate the differences one finds in title pages and book cover art across various historical and modern editions. The first known edition, published in 1600, is entitled: *The most excellent Historie of the Merchant of Venice. With the extreame crueltie of* Shylocke *the Iewe towards the sayd Merchant, in cutting a iust pound of his fleshe and the obtayning of* Portia *by the choyse of three chests* (1600: Shakespeare Documented). Later, in Shakespeare's First Folio, published posthumously in 1623, the title has been shortened to *The Merchant of Venice*, and the play is no longer advertised as a 'historie', but generically catalogued as a comedy (1623: Sig. A5 r). Students can go out into the wild and select examples they find intriguing or contradictory and explain how and what caught their attention. They may also compare their findings to the edition they will read from in class. How does the cover or title page portray the main chararacters? What does such imagery suggest about how stereotypes are created over time? This activity provides an opportunity for teachers to introduce students to the play's painful portrayals of anti-Semitism and prepare a foundation for respectful and nuanced class discussion.

EXPLORATION (cont.)

Question and Reflect

After gathering students' first impressions, invite them to put their deductions in conversation with Aristotle's brief and much anthologised theory of drama.[19] Aristotle argues that all drama stems from the imitation of an action (*mimesis*) and that 'Comedy aims at representing men as worse, Tragedy as better than they are in life' (2018: 224). For Aristotle, comedy is a 'low' form of entertainment and tragedy a 'high' one. Each reflects human behaviour at its worst and best, aiming to capture audiences in the 'mirror' of the theatre. Aristotle's brief definition of comedy may help students explore the contradictions in the play now known as *The Merchant of Venice*.

> Comedy is, as we have said, an imitation of characters of a lower type – not, however, in the full sense of the word bad, the ludicrous being merely a subdivision of the ugly. It consists in some defect or ugliness which is not painful or destructive. To take an obvious example, the comic mask is ugly and distorted, but does not imply pain.
>
> (2018: 244)

Does this play sound like it will meet Aristotle's criteria for comedy? Note students' preliminary hypotheses and then revisit them after reading and/or watching the play. Have their impressions changed? How might genre relate to portrayals of 'kindness' in its senses of likeness, equity and generosity (see especially: 2.1.140–178). Of humours? Of pain? Can they come up with a better way to express this play's complexity? Teachers can also adapt the foregoing questions as CPB prompts for homework, so students can collect their thoughts before class (see Section 1).

---

[19] Aristotle's theory did not circulate in Shakespeare's England; I include it here due to its widespread prominence in secondary and university curricula.

One approach to analysing the complex interactions between the *theatrum mundi*, early modern humoral theory and law in *The Merchant of Venice* is to trace how the first Act is characterised by disequilibrium. In either secular or devotional terms, the 'comedy' of life in the *theatrum mundi* emerges as the irony of humanity's struggle to achieve harmony between body and mind, or in the context of early modern medicine, to maintain an equitable humoral balance. The play's opening subverts equilibrium immediately when it introduces the titular merchant, Antonio, meditating on his melancholy:

> In sooth I know not why I am so sad.
>
> ...
>
> What stuff 'tis made of, whereof it is born,
> I am to learn;
> And such a want-wit sadness makes of me
> That I have much ado to know myself. (1.1.1–7)

Critics variously suggest that Antonio's 'unfocused depression' foreshadows his later close call with Shylock, or results from his unrequited love for Bassanio (Cohen, 2021: 40). I see both in play and would encourage students to embrace these polyvalences. But self-knowledge and identity are also at stake in these opening lines. Antonio repeats: 'I know not' (1.1.1); he has become a 'want-wit' (1.1.6); he has 'much ado to know [him]self' (1.1.7). If consciousness is situated, as Matthew Steggle suggests, 'in the warm and squishy tissues of the body and brain', then the language of the humours provides a 'potent metaphor for talking about, literally, the stream of consciousness that constitutes selfhood' (2018: 225). Antonio's melancholy, or black bile, disrupts humoral flow and consequently compromises his sense of selfhood.

For Shakespeare and his contemporaries, humoral theory forwarded a cosmological approach towards understanding the relationship of an individual's body to their health, temperament, complexion and personality. The four elements [air, fire, water and earth] corresponded to the four bodily humours [blood, phlegm, choler and melancholy]. Philip Moore's 1564 *The Hope of Health* elaborates:

> These humours, maie bee called the second elementes, or the elementes of man, for the[y] are equalle with the elementes, and the[y] haue also the qualities of Elementes. For blood is hotte and moiste, like the aire, fleume is colde and moiste, like the water: Choler is hotte and drie, like the fire, and Melancholie is cold and drie, like the yearth.'
>
> (Moore, 1564: xj).

Gail Kern Paster and others have persuasively demonstrated that 'in this cosmology, the stuff of the outside world and the stuff of the body were composed of the same elemental materials' (2004: 4). According to this model, a healthy body and a 'just' (*ad justiam*) temperament depend upon humoral balance.[20]

If this system sounds primitive, Steggle reminds us that 'in the twenty-first century we believe that everything in the material world, from dogs to pyramids, is built from varying proportions of the ninety-two (or so) elements of the periodic table' (2018: 221). The human body has long been understood as a microcosm of the elemental world, and medical astrologers extend this analogy to the macrocosm of the universe.[21] E.M.W. Tillyard cites ancient Pythagorean doctrine articulating the relation of the human to the cosmos: 'Man is called a little world . . . because he possesses all the faculties of the universe' (1959: 66). Laura Phillips develops this claim: 'The correlation between the celestial and terrestrial spheres was more than analogic; it was physical. The movements of the celestial

---

[20] For a succinct discussion of humoral theory and what constitutes a 'just' balance, see Moreau (2020).

[21] The 1572 supernova in Cassiopeia discussed in Section 1 not only changed the cosmographical landscape for Shakespeare and his contemporaries, but also has given twenty-first-century scientists important data about elements' nuclear origins. 'Nuclear' in astronomical contexts refers to the central core of celestial bodies. In 2019, NASA's CHANDRA X-ray telescope studied the remnants of what scientists now call 'Cass A' and discovered that the very same elements that contribute to the life and death cycles of stars dominate both the periodic table and the chemical composition of human bodies (NASA 2017; 2019).

spheres were thought to move the humours in the human body' (2021: np). A 'just' humoral balance emerges from the harmony between these micro- and macrocosmic worlds.

As Antonio continues, he attributes his humoral imbalance to his role in the theatre of the world. When his friends try and fail to cheer him up, Antonio replies: 'I hold the world but as the world, Gratiano, / A stage, where every man must play a part, / And mine a sad one' (1.1.79–81). One never finds out why Antonio plays such a sad part on the world's stage. As the play's titular protagonist, his melancholy is unsettling.

Portia's stage entrance similarly reflects her struggling with her role in the *theatrum mundi*: 'By my troth, Nerissa, my little body is aweary of this great world' (1.2.1–2). Portia echoes Antonio's sentiments directly before wondering at her own humoral turmoil that puts reason and emotion at odds: 'If to do were as easy as to know what were good to do ... It is a good divine that follows his own instructions ... The brain may devise laws for the blood, but a hot temper leaps o'er a cold decree' (1.2.11–17). Portia's melancholy stems from a familiar moral dilemma; she knows right from wrong but struggles with conflicting desires. She juxtaposes reason and desire with both humoural and legal language: 'laws for the blood', 'hot temper' and 'cold decree'. Portia's association of the law with both the brain and the cold casts it as phlegmatic: a wintry and wet humour that directly opposes Portia's 'hot temper', or choleric temperament associated with springtime and youth. Unlike Antonio, however, Portia's upset has a clear cause: her late father's will has engendered her disequilibrium: 'I may neither choose who I would nor refuse who I dislike, so is the will of a living daughter curbed by the will of a dead father. Is it not hard, Nerissa, that I cannot choose one, nor refuse none?' (1.2.20–22). The lottery-style casket test her father devised to select his daughter's husband seems foolproof. Each suitor must select from gold, silver and lead containers; if they choose the one containing Portia's portrait, they win her hand. The play dawdles over Portia's discomfort as suitors Morocco and Aragon take their time choosing – incorrectly. When Bassanio's turn comes, she wants him to succeed. She calls for music, a song that repeats rhymes suggesting the correct answer: lead. Portia has found her first legal loophole.[22]

Shakespeare does not construct a humoural profile for Shylock, but instead prompts questions that put pressure on the equity of historical constructions of socio-cultural identity and justice. From the outset, Shylock declares his hatred for the Christian Antonio who has damaged his business, spat on him and repeatedly called him 'dog'. Antonio crudely claims that he would do it all again, but for now, he needs to borrow money. 'Hath a dog money?' Shylock asks (1.3.119). This question is the first in an interrogation of equivalencies that drive the larger questions about the relationship between socio-cultural identity and justice in the theatre of the world.

These equivalencies intersect prominently in Shylock's demand for a pound of Antonio's flesh as his 'bond' for a loan of 3,000 ducats. Shylock offers him terms 'in kind', famously demanding 'an equal pound / Of your fair flesh, to be cut off and taken / In what part of your body pleaseth me' (1.3.148–150). Later, when Salarino asks what Antonio's flesh will be good for, Shylock replies: 'To bait fish withal, if it will feed nothing else, it will feed my revenge' (2006a: 3.1.44–45). Teachers can excerpt these exchanges that play on the word 'kind' and ask students to Freewrite and think associatively about how many senses the word can convey. Using a dictionary can help generate nuanced associations and recognise how 'kindness' signals not only equivalency, but carries polysemous associations with anthropology, mercenary exchange and generosity that are very much in conversation with the play's investment in the construction of Jewish, Christian and gendered identities. The following activity provides an opportunity to explore Shylock's theory of equivalencies and to reflect upon how one's sense of self and identity evolves in relation to one's socio-cultural status and environment.

---

[22] See also Shakespeare, ed. Drakakis (2010: 3.2.63–65, n.64).

EXPLORATION: SCORING SHYLOCK'S SPEECH

Getting Started

Invite students to 'score' or mark-up Shylock's 'Hath not a Jew eyes' speech to read aloud and record. This activity was inspired by Valerie Clayman Pye's excellent model in *Unearthing Shakespeare* (2017: 153–182). Here I have simplified her approach to make this exercise more flexible for classroom use. I like paper and coloured pens/markers/crayons for this activity, but it can also easily be set-up for GoogleDocs and completed individually or collaboratively.

Ask students to mark up the following elements:

1. Structure of the verse/prose: How does the speech move? Where might you pause to emphasise logic or pathos?
2. Development of thoughts through repetition and concatenation (the linking of words together).
3. Language/literary devices: Teachers might select a few focus terms that align with their unit goals.
4. Balance: How are ideas formulated and considered?

Question and Reflect

After students have 'scored' the speech, ask them to read aloud or to record themselves speaking it with *feeling*. Paying close attention to linguistic progression can be a powerful activity that helps students empathise with Shylock's character and recognise how the play's language reflects its driving themes. This activity can also serve as a Commonplace Book Prompt, inviting students to reflect on their experiences recording their readings and to pose questions for class discussion.

Just as the interacting elements of the human body must maintain balance to be healthy, so too the law. In *The Merchant of Venice*, Rebecca Lemon recognises 'the impossibility of invoking "law" as a stable category. To speak of "law" as a singular force is to collapse a set of diverse and often competing practices' (Lemon, 2012: 557). 'Justice' – then as now – is comprised of three key elements: the law itself, equity (fairness) and mercy (clemency). Like the bodily humours, these elements must be held in balance to deliver justice.

When Shylock refuses to accept late payment and resists Portia-as-Balthazar's eloquent argument in favour of mercy (4.1.187–209), she does not simply pay back his mercilessness in kind, but 'betters the instruction' (3.1.60). Portia's disquisition on mercy, much like Lorenzo's on the 'music of the spheres' that follows (5.1.61–73), may have flattered some in Shakespeare's Elizabethan audiences who gazed in this mirror and saw their cultural superiority reflected in Shylock's sentencing. But modern audiences should not be swayed so easily. Portia's merciless hypocrisy and Lorenzo's condescending cruelty toward Jessica cannot be overlooked (5.1.77–95).[23] Teachers can pair these scenes and ask students to analyse what shared points of contact emerge among bodies, law and harmony. How does the language of 'justice' take shape? Who determines what is 'just'? This play also raises a question about the role of expertise in delivering judicial equity. After all, the 'judge' in Shylock's case has been impersonated by a young woman with a vested interest in the trial's outcome. What consequences might this manipulation of the legal system generate for Venetian justice in the future?

When Portia fails to move Shylock, she pivots from an appeal to pathos and overgoes him in logos. Lemon traces how Portia fraudulently 'hooks' Shylock 'into a method of judicial interpretation that apparently favours him; but her method merely presages the radical literalism (flesh but no blood) that she will use against him in establishing the contract as unenforceable and forfeit'. This 'kangaroo court' invokes archaic Venetian laws to strip Shylock of his wealth, home and living before forcing his

---

[23] Dennis Austin Britton further and rightly insists that Lorenzo's lines here contradict Jessica's conversion (2021: 119–121).

conversion to Christianity (Lemon, 2012: 566). Broken contracts abound when Antonio and Gratiano are tricked out of their wedding rings only to have them restored amidst bawdy sexual innuendo in the final scene.[24] Lemon's observation that Shakespeare offers 'a catalogue of the law's prejudices, from construction to application to interpretation' in Act 4 that extends through the play's conclusion is spot on (2012: 566).

The Merchant of Venice is a difficult play to teach, but to my mind, that is why it should be taught. One cannot let Shakespeare off the hook for his anti-Semitic portrayals of the Jewish characters in this play. Instead, we can ask questions to better understand where the playwright was coming from, and how religious and racial prejudices have become institutionally ingrained and persist. Does the humoral imbalance that characterises Antonio and Portia from the play's outset signal a schism in the dominant culture that requires resolution or condemnation? Although Shylock craves 'the law', was its final adjudication representative of justice? What distinguishes the Christian characters from the Jewish ones? Shakespeare's intersecting frames that network bodily humours, identity and justice in the theatre of the world simultaneously generate distance and nuance from which to explore the complex adjudications of law, equity and mercy then and now. These questions surrounding cultural constructions of identity are prominent also in *Othello*, and the following discussion and activities can help students further explore Shakespeare's complex characterisations.

'Heaven is my judge': Othello

Othello's driving question is: how can one recognise the difference between 'seeming' and 'being' in the theatre of the world? This is a big question for anyone to consider, let alone students navigating what Thomas P. Mackey and Trudi E. Jacobson have declared 'a post-truth world' (2019; see Prologue). Unlike *As You Like It* and *The Merchant of Venice*, *Othello's* dramatisation of the 'theatre of the world' is not transparently obvious, but it is no less present. This play sets out twenty-six variants of the word 'world' and sixty-eight of 'heaven'. According to Open Source Shakespeare, 'heaven'

---

[24] For an accessible discussion about this 'ring scene' and its nuances, see Lanier (2019, 144–153).

is nowhere repeated more in his entire corpus (my count; 2003).[25] Throughout *Othello*, both the 'world' and 'heaven' flash in and out of comprehension, rarely holding fast to a singular connotation. One finds the hierarchy of judgement associated with the *theatrum mundi* dissolving amidst shifting micro- and macrocosmic perspectives that radically complicate discerning appearance from reality.

This subsection explores the theatre of the world from the perspectives of cartographic ethnography, optics and cosmography to explore how identities and worlds are not essential entities, but are socially and politically constructed. The following discussion and classroom activities can help students generate historical and contemporary perspectives surrounding these socio-political constructions. In closing, I invite comparison between *Othello* and its source, Giraldi Cinthio's 'The Moor of Venice', in light of Shakespeare's departure from his predecessor's positioning of 'heaven' in relation to ultimate 'justice'. The following discussion and activities support holding multiple perspectives in view as one enacts judgement in the *theatrum mundi*.

Othello is best known as Shakespeare's greatest 'race play', but that does not mean that racial constructions in the period are black and white.[26] Since before the turn of the twenty-first century, scholars have been discussing the complexity of 'racecraft' in premodern literature. 'Racecraft' broadly describes how language and historical conditions inform racist epistemologies that wrongly posit race as determined by biology or geography. For example, Kim F. Hall observes:

> England's movement from geographic isolation into military
> and mercantile contest with other countries – sets the stage for
> the longer process by which preexisting literary tropes of
> blackness profoundly interacted with the fast-changing

---

[25] Uses of 'heaven' vary across editions; The Folger Shakespeare (2024h) numbers fifty-five instances.

[26] For excellent discussions about constructions of racial whiteness, see Paris (2021), Little, Jr. (2023) and Brown (2023).

economic relations of white Europeans and their darker 'others' during the Renaissance.   (1996: 3–4)

Ian Smith discusses how these literary tropes of blackness have been textually encoded and reified since 'the moment in early modern history when the presence of blackness, in the form and person of Africans, entered the lives of white Europeans – whether through trade, travel and exploration, immigration and, perhaps most widely, through readings of various texts' (2022: 1). Ambereen Dadabhoy and Nedda Mehdizadeh synthesise Hall's and Smith's arguments, observing that 'racial difference was key to how the Other and self were made legible, yet race was not then – as it is not now – a stable category or descriptor; it was in the process of being formed' (2023: 3).

Othello, Dadabhoy and Mehdizadeh argue, 'is doomed from the start because his race "is the cause" (5.2.1) of his and the play's bloody outcome' (2023: 3). Or, as Emma Smith declares: '*Othello* is the tragedy of a black man in a white world' (2019: 211). Again, 'blackness' is a complex construction. Ian Smith describes how blackness can operate 'too easily as the mark of unassailable difference' and further explains: 'Blackness . . . represents a body that bears within its material corporeality histories of domination, claims of illegitimacy and dispossession' (2022: 160). These histories of domination are also deeply encoded throughout premodern cartography and raise a critical question: How do representations of the 'world' contribute to racial constructions?

In the play, Othello's physical attributes are associated with stereotypes of Sub-Saharan blackness and combine with his geographical markers that magnify his cultural otherness. He is the Moor of Venice, a 'wheeling stranger' (Shakespeare, 2007b: 1.1.137) who has escaped enslavement from enemies to Christianity, and has encountered geographically diverse monstrosities, including cannibals and the terrifyingly headless Anthropophagi (1.3.136–172).[27] As Valerie Traub observes, 'Such cross-cultural encounters yield contradictory understandings of ethnicity, race, religion and nationality . . . relative degrees of civility and barbarism and the geohumoural connection between climate and complexion are projected, as they were on maps, through assumed analogies

[27] Except where otherwise indicated, citations to *Othello* hereafter follow Shakespeare, ed. K. F. Hall, 2007b and will be given by act, scene and line.

between habit and habitat' (2016: 274). 'Habit' here refers to indigenous clothing and cultural customs associated with a given place; it is a central component of anthropological ethnography. For example, when Iago says 'I know our country disposition well; / In Venice they [women] do let God see the pranks / They dare not show their husbands', we see how Venetian geography is associated with the disposition of its female inhabitants (3.3.216–218). Iago's pejorative assessment of women's 'habits' is shaped by and supports stereotypes then associated with Italian culture.

Iago projects similarly disparaging geographically-informed dispositions onto Othello. Othello's skin was black from the outset, but as the play progresses, Iago's machinations elide his appearance with the monstrous 'dispositions' of his global adventures.[28] As Michela Compagnoni contends, premodern cartographic imagery and narrative very often encode monstrosity into geographies.[29] She explains that: 'Monsters were specifically defined by the fact of living at the edges of maps but, at the same time, they refashioned those spaces as monstrous by inhabiting them ... testifying to the power politics – invariably biassed and provisional – at work' (2022: 66). Both racial otherness and monstrosity emerge as forms of culturally produced fictions that privilege dominant perspectives – in the premodern world these are white, Christian viewpoints. Debapriya Sarkar explores these constructions in the context of Shakespeare's *The Tempest* and *Antony and Cleopatra*, but the questions she raises are just as relevant for classroom approaches to *Othello*, in particular: 'How, then, might we think about natural and political geographies as mutually constituted entities that reinforce constructions of racial and cultural difference?' (2024: 56). We may think of maps as resources to get from point 'A' to point 'B', but *Othello*, like many early modern literary works, invites one to think about how they also are powerful rhetorical vehicles for conveying moral and ethical judgments.

---

[28] These geographical associations are not, as D.A. Britton contends, 'native to Othello's person ... they can work to remind us that Othello's identity is created in multiple locations' (2011: 53).

[29] Compagnoni situates her argument in relation to disability studies, reminding readers that disability and monstrosity were two sides of the same coin during early modernity (2022: 65–66).

Figure 5 Ortelius, *Theatrum Orbis Terrarum* (1606). Photograph of item held by Harvard Map Collection.

It may be telling that the theatre of the world's renewed popularity in sixteenth-century print culture coincides with a proliferation of maps, globes and atlases. Before the *theatrum mundi* metaphor made its way into the architecture of Elizabethan theatres, it was represented geographically through cartography. Abraham Ortelius' 1570 *Theatrum Orbis Terrarum*, or 'The Theatre of the World', is coextensive with precisely the kind of Ciceronian cosmographical contemplation associated with the metaphor's earlier moralising imperatives (Figure 5).[30] Ortelius presents his readers

---

[30] One may also translate Ortelius' title as the *Theatre of the Orb*.

with dual perspectives from which to contemplate what Cicero calls: 'the disposition of the whole world': The horse is created to beare & to draw: the ox to til & to labor the earth: the dog to hu[n]t and to gard the hovvs. But man to consider & contemplate with the eyes of his vnder-standing the disposition of the whole world (1601: Sig. A4 v). Cicero's and, by extension, Ortelius' anthropocentrism reflects a version of world 'order' whereby animals exist to 'labour the earth', serving the humans charged with contemplating 'the disposition of the whole world'. This hierarchy that positions humans as superior to animals and the earth itself tacitly underscores how the terrestrial world was viewed as a way station to divine judgement.

Ortelian hierarchies are not limited to elevating humans at the expense of animals and the planet, but are deeply invested in exalting the virtues of Northern Europeans to the detriment of other peoples and places. Students can contemplate the title page and brainstorm what kind of visual argument it conveys.[31] Even a cursory examination of the allegorical figures personifying earth's continents on *Theatrum Orbis Terrarum's* title page can incite classroom conversations about constructions of culture and race. Ortelius sets his stage with a markedly Christian Europa surmounting a portico supported by persons ethnographically marked as Asia and Africa. The space beneath the 'stage' is populated by a native American depicted as a savage, holding a decapitated head – clearly of European origin – victoriously by the hair. This unsubtle association of native costumes and indigenous customs again underscores prejudicial and blatantly racist associations conveyed through habit and habitat. In the context of the theatrical metaphor, students might think about how early modern cartography sets the stage to generate perspectives that inform both characterisation (habit) and plot (habitat).

---

[31] Maryanne Cline Horowitz's introductory chapter, 'Rival Interpretations', in *Bodies and Maps* (2021: 1–24) provides an accessible overview of continental personification and race-making.

EXPLORATION: WHAT CONSTITUTES WORLD ORDER?

The following activity has several parts that can be taught separately or together to engage students in collaborative, complex and compassionate thinking about worldmaking and who gets to do it.

Getting Started

1. Ask students to Freewrite about what 'world order' means to them. They may work individually or collaboratively in an anonymous, shared GoogleDoc. Ask students to identify what conceptual patterns emerge.
2. Engage in Ortelian-inspired cosmographical contemplation. Divide the class into small groups and assign each a different 'world map'. Ortelius' maps and descriptions are freely available for download from the Folger Shakespeare Library Digital Collections (https://digital collections.folger.edu/). So too is John Speed's 1631 *Prospect of the Most Famous Parts of the World*. Here, students might explore how Speed's illustration of the African continent literally marginalises non-European cultures and hints at the monstrosities that populate 'The Aethiopian Ocean'. How do maps convey socio-cultural assessments of terrestrial geography?
3. How might continental prejudices still inform cartography today? Invite students to compare images of Mercator-inspired maps with the Gall-Peters Projection; these are quite different, especially from Pacific and Atlantic perspectives.[32]

---

[32] Teachers might also curate a collection of historical maps for this activity. See also Houston's short essay and video clips in *The Conversation*: 'Five Maps that will change how you see the world' (2017).

> **EXPLORATION (cont.)**
>
> ### Question and Reflect
>
> Instructors might ask: What is the central focus in each 'world' map? What is marginalised? How does geography emerge as a subjective discipline? Students may also Freewrite and reflect upon how their geographical locations have informed their personal identities. This activity again fosters habits of mind that consider multiple perspectives before generating conclusions.

Maps in Shakespeare's day and our own aspire to represent spatial forms found on earth and in the cosmos. The problem is, as Traub remarks, that an essential disparity exists between perception and representation. Much as we cannot see the earth's sphere in its entirety, it is impossible to represent a three-dimensional object accurately in two dimensions (Traub, 2016: 267). This perplexity raises the question: is there an inherent schism between 'seeming' and 'being'? Taking maps as exemplary, how might one know the difference between what is represented and what truly exists? Perhaps the best one may do is to try and hold two perspectives in 'view' simultaneously. Again, parallax can provide an analogical frame that supports juxtaposing concrete and abstract concepts, and to recognise that any assessment of 'character' (or an object in space) will depend on the viewer's position in the world (see Section 1). A parallax approach can help students realise that what *seems* to them might *be* to someone else, and that both propositions might be true at the same time. 'Truth', Jonathan Bate rightly argues, 'is not singular' in Shakespeare's plays; that is not to say that it does not exist, but is relative to the conditions of perception and performance (1998: 327–330).

For Ortelius, 'eyes' are a dominant metaphor for knowledge-making; his illustrated geographies invite contemplation of space and scale. Each map is accompanied by a commentary about the demographics of a given region, as well as its crops and economies. John Gillies elaborates Ortelius' perspective: 'Geography . . . is imagined as an all-seeing *eye* commanding the spatial and temporal immensities of history [;] the map is imagined as a *glass* or means by which the god's eye view of geography is accommodated to the limited perspective of human sight' (2016: 71). But this 'god's eye view of geography' is also a metaphor and cannot accommodate the limited perspective of human sight. Although maps and three-dimensional globes repeatedly aimed to render the 'disposition of the whole world', concurrent studies of perspective and optics suggest instead that our worldviews emerge from the 'visual turbulence' that characterises perspective and multiplies *ad infinitum* through space and time (Clark, 2007: 5). To this day, epistemologies of visual cognition, much like their linguistic equivalents, emerge through relativity (Clark, 2007: 5–7).

Early modern advances in optics and perspective contribute to the *theatrum mundi's* evolution from a moralising metaphor to one that reflects scepticism about mythologies of world 'order' and ideals of justice. As Stuart Clark observes, 'Human subjects "make" the objects they perceive, fashioning them out of the qualities that belong intrinsically to perception, not to the objects themselves' (2007: 14). For example, Hans Holbein's painting *The Ambassadors* vivifies early modern thinking with perspective in the theatre of the world (National Gallery, 1533). The maps, globes, astrolabes, books and musical instruments in the painting signal intellectual aspiration, the hope of understanding the world and cosmos. The large anamorphic skull that can be seen only at an angle functions as a *memento mori*, a reminder of death designed – like early iterations of the *theatrum mundi* topos – to inspire virtue in this world by reminding viewers that judgement awaits in the next.

Of course, these chimerical phenomena are not limited to painting, but are vividly realised in the theatre. Wendy Beth Hyman reminds us of drama's origins in the 'amphitheatre', etymologically a place of 'seeing both ways' (2022: 402). The amphitheatre's essential duality also parallels Aristotle's theory of drama itself as generically mimetic. That is to say that drama imitates, and thus is always already a 'seeming'. 'Being' is an interpretive challenge.

Throughout his plays, Shakespeare repeatedly interrogates the horizons of 'seeming' and 'being'; Othello's obsession about 'ocular proof' offers a case in point (3.3.377). One might pause to consider how the horizon itself is a matter of perception, defined as 'that part of the earth's surface visible from a given point of view; the line at which the earth and sky appear to meet' (*OED*, horizon, n.1a). Like the amphitheatre, a horizon looks both ways, its vanishing point signals 'the representation of space that is oriented in relation to its absence' (Hyman, 2022: 403). In *Othello*, this phenomenon of absence is prominent, especially in Iago's suggestive narrative that reorients the loss of Desdemona's handkerchief as 'proof' of her infidelity. Iago's narratives of *seeming* have been transformed into *being*, rather, perception has become reality.[33]

Othello's driving interest in optics and the role of perception in identity construction and virtue is partly indebted to his source, Cinthio's *Gli Hecatommithi*, 'The Moor of Venice' (2000). Shakespeare follows Cinthio's plot quite closely, and echoes his predecessor's deployment of visual and linguistic turbulence. Yet Shakespeare departs from his source's moralising dramatisations of the *theatrum mundi* in his representations of heaven and ultimate justice.

Students can productively compare and contrast the two narratives to think about how Shakespeare innovates on his sources. Cintho's narrative may be summarised as follows. A Venetian lady 'Disdemona' (Shakespeare's Desdemona) marries a 'Moor' (Shakespeare's Othello) with whom she is deeply in love. Cinthio's 'Ensign' (Shakespeare's Iago) serves the Moor, but lusts after Disdemona. He tries to seduce her with no success and convinces himself that she must prefer the 'Captain' (Shakespeare's Cassio), failing to perceive that she truly loves her husband. Jealousy drives the Ensign to persuade the Moor that Disdemona has been unfaithful. He contrives the loss of Disdemona's handkerchief to use as proof and convinces the Moor to murder his wife, and to make it look like an accident. The murder is grisly. The Ensign later will be tortured and killed for another crime, but the narrator suggests these are just deserts for what he has done to the Moor and his wife. The Moor himself mourns his wife's loss desperately, but his penalty awaits: 'Heaven, the just regarder of all hearts, willed not that so wicked a deed should go unpunished' (2020: 10). Following a few more plot twists, the Signoria of Venice try the 'barbarian' Moor and torture him, but he

---

[33] See also Dennis Austin Britton (2011: 42–44).

will not confess. Ultimately, Disdemona's kinfolk kill him and the story concludes by moralising: 'Thus did Heaven avenge the innocence of Disdemona' (2020: 11). First written in 1565, Cinthio's *Gli Hecatommthi* retains a cosmographical perspective that fixes the Heavens to represent a sense of judicial equity. By contrast, Shakespeare's *Othello* disintegrates associations between 'heaven' and 'justice'.

Iago is the first in *Othello* to link heaven with judgement. Because he is the play's amoral villain, its associations with integrity are immediately subverted:

> Heaven is my judge, not I for love and duty,
> But seeming so, for my peculiar end:
> For when my outward action doth demonstrate
> The native act and figure of my heart
> In compliment extern, 'tis not long after
> But I will wear my heart upon my sleeve
> For daws to peck at: I am not what I am.
>
> (2007b: 1.1.59–67)

Iago's 'Heaven' is a supremely ambiguous judge. It is unclear whether he aims to dupe some kind of divine judge, or if 'heaven's' judicial powers have dissolved, leaving nothing to fear. Teachers might usefully substitute the word 'heaven' for 'world' in Section 1's Exploration: 'What constitutes a world?' Additionally, they may ask students to test different connotations that emerge from the following examples, or from using a concordance or other searchable text:[34]

> If after every tempest come such calms,
> May the winds blow till they have wakened death,
> And let the labouring bark climb hills of seas
> Olympus high, and duck again as low

---

[34] Open Source Shakespeare provides an easy to use concordance. One also can download searchable editions of the play from The Folger Shakespeare.

As hell's from heaven! (Shakespeare, 2024h: 2.1.201–205)
Now by yond marble heaven (Shakespeare, 2024h: 3.3.521–522)

If heaven would make me such another world
Of one entire and Perfect chrysolite,
I'd not have sold her for it (Shakespeare, 2024h: 5.2.175–177)

Throughout Shakespeare's works 'heaven' refers both to a realm of divine justice (Christian or pagan) and to the cosmos. If one approaches Iago's statement in the context of the *theatrum mundi*, one might read the heavenly audience as capable of judgement, but perhaps as too apathetic or too dull-witted to discern between seeming and being, between good and bad actors.

EXPLORATION: THE FOUR POINTS OF CHARACTER ANALYSIS

The Four Points of Character Analysis is a deceptively simple activity that can help students generate novel perspectives to think about identity construction and character development.[35] This activity is suited to independent or small group work.

Getting Started

Task students with first picking a character before addressing the following questions and supporting their deductions with textual evidence:

1. What does your character say?
2. What does your character do?
3. What do other characters say about your character?
4. What do other characters do in similar circumstances?

---

[35] This activity reframes a lesson given by J.J.M. Tobin in courses taught at University of Massachusetts, Boston.

> ### EXPLORATION (cont.)
>
> Searchable texts facilitate this activity and teachers also might choose to coordinate these queries with data available in The Folger Shakespeare API (Application Program Interface) Tools. Here, one may select from a variety of functions designed to generate diverse perspectives from which to 'see' a given play in a new light (Shakespeare, 2024). At the bottom of the page, one can find a guide: 'The API in Action: The Four Points of Character Analysis' (Bennett, 2019). This set of slides guides teachers through using selected API functions, including 'Text by character', 'witScript' (witness script), 'Text, minus a character's' and 'Character Chart' that align to each of The Four Points prompts.
>
> ### Question and Reflect
>
> Once students have gathered their data about characters, invite them to share how their views about the character may have changed. What internal and external factors might contribute to identity construction and character development? Teachers can also ask students how they curate their own identities on social media: what is in their control? What lies out of it? Do we have opportunities to be more compassionate in our assessments of others?

In the context of the *theatrum mundi*, *Othello* finds cartographical perceptions of 'habit' (ethnography) and 'habitat' (geography) operating across both macro- and microcosmic scales of relation. Students can approach these concepts by thinking about how they might analogise literary conventions like 'character' and 'setting'. Close analysis of the interactions between geographies and identities are, as Iago demonstrates, very often constructed by distorted perceptions and prejudices. At the same time, one finds Shakespeare asking: what constitutes the identity of the 'theatre' of the 'world'? If our planetary world's 'habits' are determined by its 'habitat', then how do our worlds emerge in relation to an infinite theatrical universe? This brief survey of Shakespeare's thematic exploration of the theatre of the world in *As You Like It*, *The Merchant of Venice* and *Othello* aims to liberate the metaphor from cliché. It seeks to inspire teachers and students to join Shakespeare in questioning the factors that shape protean perspectives on justice, identity and perception. Next, I examine Shakespeare's formal experiments reconstructing these dynamic perspectives in the context of *A Midsummer Night's Dream*, *Henry V* and *Hamlet*.

3 Formal Explorations of the Theatre of the World

When Shakespeare contemplated the night sky, he apprehended a universe pulsing with possibility. People had long speculated that the moon and the stars, then also synonymous with planets, were inhabited.[36] So far, this Element has examined how Shakespeare raises and develops broad themes associated with the theatre of the world. Next, it explores how Shakespeare formally calls into being world-systems that alter both the conditions of playing and the players themselves in *A Midsummer Night's Dream*, *Henry V* and *Hamlet*. James Shapiro has observed that these works, roughly contemporaneous with one another, 'show signs of a struggle ... to forge a new kind of drama by resisting the tendency to handle conflict in conventional ways' (2006: 126). These plays suggest that their aims are not to 'handle' conflict, but to dramatise it, disrupting linear epistemologies and raising questions about the complex conditions from which 'theatre' and 'world' take shape over time and at scale. The following discussions and Explorations encourage students to practise thinking from perspectives that can feel distant or inconsequential in their daily lives, but that may be more closely related than they think.

'Mazèd World': A Midsummer Night's Dream

In *A Midsummer Night's Dream*, audiences find themselves in a time-wrinkled Athens populated by a mash-up of historical and fictional characters. They are then transported to a magical forest governed by capricious fairies where they

---

[36] See Włodarczyk et al. (2021: 408–409).

discover that Queen Titania and King Oberon's disputes have had disastrous impacts upon the environment (Shakespeare, 2024a: 2.1.84–120).[37] Worlds, stages, settings and time are foregrounded in this dramatisation of plural world orders. This section provides two Explorations designed to help students apprehend the complexity of Titania's 'mazèd world' (2.1.116). The first invites students to investigate how the play dramatises complex timescapes and settings as it multiplies world-systems and interpretive possibilities. The second provides a classroom adaptation of Urie Bronfenbrenner's twentieth-century Ecological Systems Theory (EST). Bronfenbrenner visualises a cosmological analogue that supports recognising how interacting socio-political systems inform an individual's development. EST lends itself directly to studying literary characters, but here I refigure it to de-centre humans so students may perceive how system interactions generate consequences that may not be immediately apparent, but are no less impactful. These Explorations can generate insight and context for contemplating one's role in the *theatrum mundi* from micro- and macroscopic perspectives over time and at scale.

Thinking with scale in the classroom affords an opportunity to disrupt linear approaches to classroom knowledge-making. 'Scale' not only describes 'difference' but embodies it etymologically and as a homophone. From the Latin *scala*, or ladder, 'scale' initially conveys vertical hierarchies that are soon disrupted by the word's polysemousness. One finds the 'scales of justice' weighing in to measure relative balances of law, equity, and mercy, even as the phrase slithers into biological connotations, describing the outer 'skin' of fish, reptiles, and some invertebrates.[38] At the same time, musical scales invite thinking about *arrangement* and can set the stage for comprehending what Timothy Clark describes as scale's inevitable *derangement*. For Clark, 'derangement' describes a loss of 'linguistic and intellectual proportion' when people speak of vast concepts like the environment (2012: 150–151).[39]

---

[37] Citations to *MND* hereafter follow Shakespeare, eds. B. Mowat, P. Werstine, M. Poston & R. Niles, 2024a, and will be given by act, scene and line.

[38] For a discussion about scale and monstrosity, see Baer (2019, np).

[39] This loss is similar to the essential disparity between perception and representation discussed earlier in the context of geography and *Othello*; see also Traub, 2016: 267.

Humans most often perceive scalar distance – or guess at it – through time.[40] We experience time as linear, but the way humans mark it depends upon their location and perspective. Today, scientists debate how to measure time, specifically in relation to geological ages. The Holocene Epoch (Greek for 'entirely recent') that started 11,650 years ago recently has given way to the not unproblematic designation of the Anthropocene (*Anthropos* is Greek for 'human'). The 'Anthropocene' marks the moment when human signatures emerge in the geological record (Lewis and Maslin, 2015: 171).[41] This geological shift results from human activities like agriculture, deforestation, naval exploration and mining, from wars fought on land and at sea, plus the waste generated from these endeavours.

James C. Scott makes a strong case for recognising a 'thin Anthropocene' emerging from early hominid settlements around 12,000 BCE that gave rise to many unintended environmental consequences long before the 'thick Anthropocene' that would date from geological radioactivity resulting from the first nuclear bomb blast (2017: 3, 19). Scott's recognition of pluralised human signatures permits including another proposed start date for the Anthropocene: the 1610 'Orbis spike'.[42] The Orbis spike marks historically low levels of CO_2 that are concurrent with European colonial expansion in the Americas, and the deaths of millions of Indigenous people (Lewis and Maslin, 2015: 174). Population estimates in the Americas before 1492 range from 54 to 61 million people. By 1650, these 'numbers rapidly declined to a minimum of about 6 million people by 1650 via exposure to diseases carried by Europeans, plus war, enslavement and famine' (Lewis and Maslin, 2015: 175). Travis Weiland remarks that the Orbis spike 'highlights power relations between peoples and their impact on

---

[40] This Element's accompanying film supports introducing students to scalar thinking. See 'This Universal Theatre' (Video 1).

[41] The term 'Anthropocene' is problematic because it describes the impact of a subset of humanity. Andrew Baldwin and Bruce Erikson follow several predecessors re-situating the Anthropocene as an effect of white European colonialism (2020: 3–11).

[42] For an excellent discussion about pluralising the Anthropocene, see Mentz (2019: 1–14). For an overview of catastrophising impulses, see Steffen (2023: 6–14).

the natural world. It also makes explicit the insidiousness of colonialism and its influence on the world' (2022: 186). Western-centric, dominant culture narratives frame early modern exploration as a celebrated endeavour, but with scalar perspectives afforded by hindsight, one may recognise how it also generated negative consequences for nearly all our planetary systems.

A Midsummer Night's Dream provides an ideal opportunity for students to think about how international power relations and state-sanctioned acquisitiveness can impact both fictional and actual worlds. Titania directly recognises how her and Oberon's 'forgeries of jealousy' contribute directly to what we now call climate change:

> These are the forgeries of jealousy;
>
> ...
>
> And thorough this distemperature we see
> The seasons alter: hoary-headed frosts
> Fall in the fresh lap of the crimson rose,
> And on old Hiems' thin and icy crown
> An odorous chaplet of sweet summer buds
> Is, as in mockery, set. The spring, the summer,
> The childing autumn, angry winter, change
> Their wonted liveries, and the mazèd worldBy
>   their increase now knows not which is which.
> And this same progeny of evils comes
> From our debate, from our dissension;
> We are their parents and original. (2.1.84–120)

Titania directly attributes this rebellion of the natural world to her contentious relationship with Oberon. Since antiquity, humans have blamed natural disasters on divine displeasure with earthly events (Dilek and Kahya, 2023: 819–828). Titania's speech suggests that in Shakespeare's time some blamed monarchs – those positioned as God's representatives on earth – for climate disasters, plague and pestilence. As E.M.W. Tillyard observes, 'it is a commonplace that the order of the state duplicates the order of the microcosm' (1959: 88). That is not to say that people thought monarchs controlled the weather, but it was plausible to many that a ruler's leadership had displeased their God. Shakespeare's quarrelling fairies may be seen to either satirise superstitions about rulers' influences on the natural world, or perhaps to underscore them. Either way, in a political climate of rigorous censorship, the fairy world provides a foil from which the play can engage with topical events from a position of relative safety.

The play's fantastical setting also appears to question whether the natural world – in fairyland, or in Elizabethan England – adheres to some kind of orderly cosmological logic. Bottom's dream suggests not. Awakening from a post-coital nap, Bottom's bestial encounter with Titania seems unreal: 'The eye of man hath not heard, the ear of man hath not seen, man's hand is not able to taste, his tongue to conceive, nor his heart to report what my dream was' (4.1.220–224). Bottom's synaesthesia upon emerging from his drugged encounters with Titania is not just comedic; it enacts how dreams mirror disordered sensory and chronological information.

Shakespeare's portrayal of dreamscapes adapts Thomas Nashe's dream theories on offer in *The Terrors of the Night*. Here, Nashe associates the elemental collisions that combined to create our planet with those that engender dreams: 'No such figure as the first Chaos whereout the world was extraught, as our dreames in the night. In them all states, all sexes, all places are confounded and meete together' (1966: 356.11–14). In one sense, the modernised form of 'meet' means to encounter, but it also works as a homonym for 'mete', meaning to apportion reward or punishment (*OED*, mete, v.1), and as 'meat' or food for thought and for dreams. Bottom's muddled dream directly enacts how 'all states, all sexes, all places are confounded and meete together' and raises a question that was as pressing for Shakespeare and his contemporaries as it is now: Does the disorder one experiences in dreams reflect that in the cosmos? According to Pythagoras in ancient Greece, 'kosmos' synonymised the 'universe' with 'order'. (*OED*, cosmos, n.1, Etymology). Tillyard repeatedly asserts that 'the conception of order is so taken for granted, so much a part of the collective mind' of Elizabethans. But he struggles with the *disorder* one finds in Shakespeare's and his contemporaries' works and tries to explain it away as a kind of 'queer regulation' (1959: 9). Tillyard's insistence on the Elizabethan belief in cosmic order seems like wishful thinking, especially when there is so much evidence to the contrary.

EXPLORATION: TIMESCAPES AND SETTINGS

This Exploration links time and space to help students envision *A Midsummer Night's Dream* as a constellation of worlds, each adhering to different standards of equity and justice. Students will discover how the Athenian characters and Puck carry with them multiple identities that are forged in both the play's action and its historical intertexts. This 'collect, reflect and question' activity can help students query how and what intertextual allusions *formally* contribute to the subtext of a literary work. They'll need to think associatively, creatively and critically as they gather and analyse the following information.

Getting Started

Assign each student, pair or group one character to research according to their 'State, Sex and Place' (see Nashe mentioned previously):

State: Social status (race, class), Species (human, part-human, divine, bestial, part-bestial), Fictional, Historical

Sex: Gender(s), Sexual orientation(s)

Place: Time, Geographical or Cosmographical coordinates, Fiction, History

This activity can easily be scaled to students' skill levels. Beginners might start with basic resources like Behind the Name (https://www.behindthename.com/), Online Etymology Dictionary (https://www.etymonline.com/) or Wikipedia. Other helpful open-source databases include Mythopedia (https://mythopedia.com/) and The British Library (https://www.bl.uk/). Students can gather data in a GoogleDoc, or create CPB slides (see Section 2). Advanced students might trace these characters to their sources directly and put these different works in conversation. Helpful databases for this approach include Internet Archive (https://archive.org/details/texts) and

EXPLORATION (cont.)

Perseus Digital Library (https://www.perseus.tufts.edu/hopper/).[43] One aim is for students to recognise how main characters like Theseus and Hippolyta have various narratives attached to their mythological characters, which intertextually challenge straightforward approaches to the conditions of their marriage. At the same time, they may consider how the characters' assignments to diverse time periods complicate representations of time in the play.[44]

Question and Reflect

After examining their findings, students might come together to visualise (timeline, map and sketch) how each character emerges from different times and places. Students can approach these overlapping timescapes and settings by asking: Do the characters in Shakespeare's play gain or lose a sense of individuality in relation to their historical predecessors? How do characters' histories impact their roles in the play? How do these allusions add texture to the play's plot, themes or genre? Once students have a chance to sit with the vastity of Shakespeare's narrative constellation, they can actively contemplate how the foregoing elements are 'confounded'.

---

[43] Students also can explore the essential arbitrariness of measuring time itself. Until 1582, Europe and England used the Julian calendar, a 365-day solar calendar from the Roman Empire. Due to inaccuracies in the solar year, calendar dates shifted. In 1582, the Catholic Church reformed the calendar to align dates like Easter with Biblical narratives, and European countries adopted it. However, Protestant England refused, creating a ten-day difference between dates in England and the Continent. See also MacInnes, *English Calendar* (2023).

[44] Some might want to explore the textual crux one finds surrounding the moon's progress in Theseus' speech. Most editors have followed Q2 wherein Theseus laments 'how slow / This old Moone wanes' (Kennedy et al., 2025: 6–7). But the play's 'four days' are compressed into three, and the moon never wanes. Might there be a case to make for the first quarto's use of 'waves' in lieu of 'wanes'? What might this say about the play's timescales?

One funny-not-funny question the foregoing activity raises is: Are people essentially interchangeable? Some have argued that the lovers in the Forest are barely distinguishable from one another (Smith, 2021: 87). But from the scale of the *theatrum mundi*, this question can be disturbing. Are people judged based on our individual merit? Or are we generalised into communities, social classes, generational age groups or species that are determined by time and place? Students might reflect upon how they are talked about as 'Gen Z' or as 'Gen Alpha'. Are the generalisations applied to them fair? One big question arises: what implications might these formally overlapping elements have for the concepts of justice and equity in the *theatrum mundi* across time and space?

Titania's 'mazèd world' in *A Midsummer Night's Dream* exemplifies the scale effects that emerge from asynchronously interacting world-systems, specifically those resulting from her conflict with Oberon. This 'mazèd world' emerges partly from meteorological and cosmological disruptions that mirror those actually impacting the northern hemisphere from the middle of the sixteenth century to the turn of the seventeenth. Extreme weather patterns may have favoured England when defeating the Spanish Armada in 1588, but in the mid-1590s, they led to ruined crops and famine for three years running – and that on the heels of plague and conflicts arising from European colonial expansion. How can teachers help students apprehend these moving pieces and their consequences?

At this point, I would like to introduce Urie Bronfenbrenner's Ecological Systems Theory (EST) as an approach for analysing the roles of both human and non-human actors in the theatre of the world. Bronfenbrenner's concentric model of an individual's interacting ecosystems resonates directly with those of the early modern cosmos (see Stern et al., 2021: figure 2, 12). This striking if serendipitous similarity urges one to think about how approaches toward tracing the complexity of human development analogise how early modern astronomers grappled with shifting understandings of the universe.

Bronfenbrenner's work embraces the complex contexts that inform an individual's growth. In 1965, he co-founded the Head Start program in the United States that aimed to inject positive turbulence into low-income areas and generate educational equity. From the outset, he recognises how race and class systemically impact a child's development. He proposes EST to create an analytical framework that recognises how larger socio-political systems impact children from the outside-in and vice versa.

Interpersonal interactions remain central to current versions of EST, but I propose a flexible adaptation that can de-centralise humans. My goal is to help students realise how their understandings of the 'theatre' and the 'world' might be transformed from the perspectives of the organisms, plants, animals and elements that they interact with continually. This approach recognises 'worlds' as microcosms that emerge through interactions with larger macrocosms and supports students as they contemplate how complex systems work in literature and in life.

'Complex' in this sense does not simply mean 'complicated'. A compli*cated* system is mechanical; it may have a lot of moving pieces, but it is predictable and orderly. One of the key features of compl*exity*, a term initially borrowed from the sciences, is 'emergence'. Claire Hansen defines emergence as 'the process by which a system produces new phenomena through the interaction of its parts' (2017: 11). Bronfenbrenner was interested in how a system's 'parts', or individuals, interact with their *settings* to provoke emergence, or unpredictable outcomes. He recognises how changes in a person's sense of selfhood emerge from their interactions *with* their proximal, or adjacent, systems, including their micro-, meso-, macro-, exo- and chronosystems. Ultimately, Bronfenbrenner aspires to create a manageable framework for cognitively grappling with how human activity on a massive scale impacts an individual and vice versa (Figure 6).

What might Shakespeare's ecological systems have looked like according to this model? Let's focus on the London-based playwright in 1595, one proposed date for the composition of *A Midsummer Night's Dream*. Broadly speaking, Shakespeare's *microsystem* would include his direct interactions with others in a given setting. For Bronfenbrenner, this setting is usually the home environment. In 1595, Shakespeare lived in St. Helen's parish, Bishopsgate. [45] He likely

[45] Students can explore Shakespeare's London via the Map of Early Modern London (Jenstad, 2006). For video research tutorials, see Jeromski (2021). Internet Shakespeare Editions provides an accessible resource for studying events in Shakespeare's life by date; see 'Years 1595–1596' (2023). For a detailed account of events, see Colthorpe (2017).

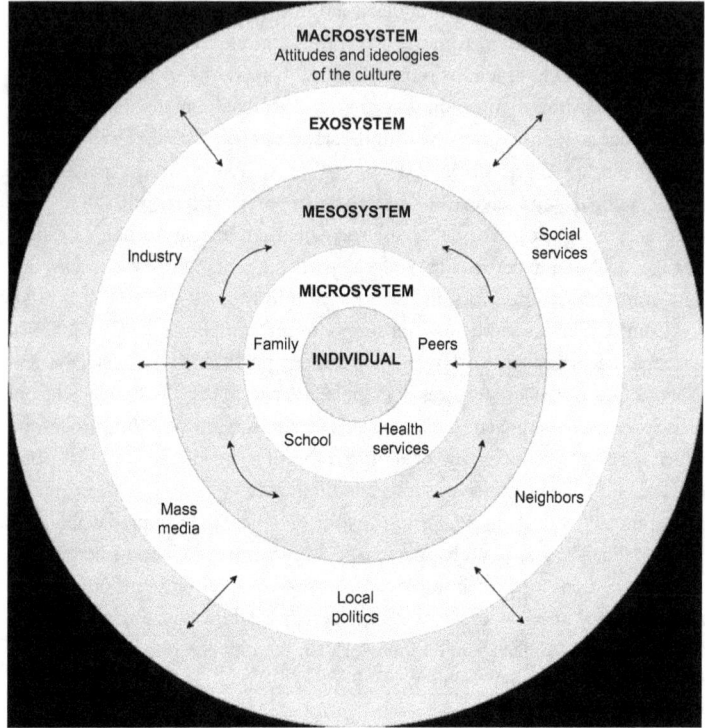

Figure 6 A figure showing Bronfenbrenner's EST (Abbeyelder, 2022).

rented a room in a boarding house where he would have known his fellow residents and taken meals. Although his family may not have been present, they also should be considered part of his immediate setting. The next sphere is the *mesosystem*; this includes the interactions between two different settings that contain the focal subject. Shakespeare's mesosystem would include those in his microsystem, as well as the microsystems of those he interacted with, including his fellow actors and managers of The Lord Chamberlain's Men and his family in Stratford. Next, the *exosystem* recognises how interacting social and political systems affect the focal subject. For example, poor harvests in the 1590s had led to exponential increases in food prices. In June 1595, anti-alien (immigrant) riots broke out in London, so too protests against rising fish and butter prices that resulted in Queen Elizabeth issuing a proclamation banning large gatherings in London (Colthorpe, 2017: 1595). Moving outward to Shakespeare's *macrosystem*, one would find the systemic ideologies of cultures and subcultures that form his socio-political ecosystem. The Protestant Reformation and tensions throughout Europe would figure largely here. So too would colonial explorations like those of Sir Walter Raleigh to Guiana and South America. Shakespeare's *chronosystem* would comprise the interactions among these ecosystems and the emergent changes they mutually produce over time. One might ask students: How might the consequences created by Shakespeare's interacting ecosystems have informed his playwriting? How might these systems continue to exert influence now?

EXPLORATION: MAPPING ECOSYSTEMS

This Exploration provides a framework for thinking critically and creatively about how ecological systems interact to produce unpredictable results in the theatre of the world. Students analyse how a focal entity – an *actor* – interacts with both their immediate settings and larger interacting systems with which they share proximal links. The following sample model redefines Bronfenbrenner's terminology in the context of the *theatrum mundi*. It aims to help students think across time *and* space as they analyse system interactions.

Getting Started

This sample activity explores ecological systems from the perspective of Corn in Titania's reflection upon the 'mazèd world' (The Folger Shakespeare, 2024a: 2.1.84–116).

1. What is the Focal Entity?

> *The focal entity analogises the role of the 'actor' in the theatre of the world. They both influence and are influenced by their surroundings.*
>
> Corn in Titania's speech (see 2.1.97)

EXPLORATION (cont.)

2. Describe the elements that comprise the Microsystem.

   The microsystem contains the stage business or immediate environment in which the 'actor' (focal entity) is engaged.
   The ox, the field, the ploughman, rain

3. Describe the elements that comprise the Mesosystem.

   The Mesosystem analogises scenes on stage that may or may not include the 'actor,' but that represent the proximal interactions between those in different settings that both include the actor.
   Hill, dale, forest, mead, paved fountain, the rushy brook, the beached margent of the sea, the winds, contagious fogs, pelting river, the ox, sheep ('the fold'), crows, mazes, 'the human mortals' (2.1.104)

4. Describe the elements that comprise their Exosystem.

   The Exosystem represents one or more settings (setting = set of entities) *that do not involve the 'actor' as an active participant. The interactions between these settings impact the actor.*
   Titania and Oberon's 'forgeries of jealousy' (2.1.84)

5. Describe the elements that comprise their Macrosystem

   The Macrosystem comprises the cosmological environment. It can include large-scale systems and/or epistemologies that govern the formation and dissolution of communal interactions between entities. It can also represent dominant modes of knowledge-making and belief systems, empirical, philosophical or theological.
   The Moon 'governess of floods'; The seasons ('the spring, the summer, / the chiding autumn, angry winter,

EXPLORATION (cont.)

change their liveries') are not performing their 'roles' at their usual times.

6. Describe the elements that comprise their Chronosystem.

   The Chronosystem recognises how large-scale systems change over time and may subsequently transform communal patterns that impact the focal entity, both directly and by altering the configuration of ecological systems around it.

   The Moon ('pale in her anger') informs Time in the play

Question and Reflect

Synthesis and Emergence

The last step is to analyse system interactions and see what emerges.

Starting with the 'actor,' select an element from another system and analyse the interacting systems that connects them and generate questions that might help one identify possible outcomes (emergence).

Moon | Corn: How does the moon's asynchronous measure of time impact corn? How did the moon get out of synch? *Titania is associated with the moon and she is upset with Oberon.* What are the consequences? *The corn dies, and the ploughman 'loses his sweat' (labour). Animals and people go hungry.* What emerges? *Corn has adopted a different role in the theatrum mundi. It no longer represents the fruit of the ox and ploughman's labours and potential nourishment for their communities ('mortal humans') but is rotted food for crows.* What consequences does Corn's changed role generate among its proximal systems? (Figure 7).

EXPLORATION (cont.)

Question and Reflect

When I first experimented with this activity in class, students recognised how this model provided an opportunity to analyse what emerges from systemic interactions, whether they are adjacent or not. Here, thinking with the Moon and Corn led to the emergent recognition that Corn has

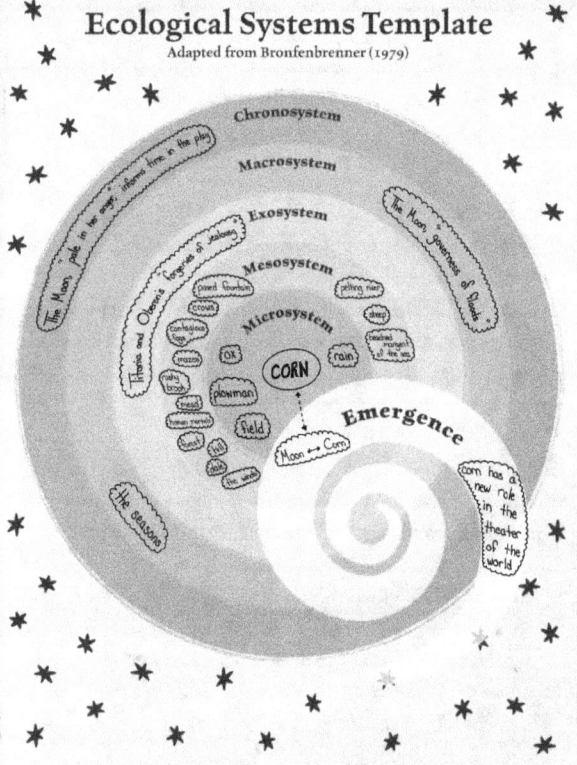

Figure 7 Sample ecosystem as conceived by Olivia Copeland.

> ### EXPLORATION (cont.)
>
> adopted a *different role* in the theatre of the world. We contemplated what consequences Corn's changed role generates among its proximal systems.
>
> Teachers may introduce beginning students to thinking with ecosystems by populating a template and skipping to the final step in this exercise, 'Synthesis and Emergence'.[46] Then they may ask students to put different systems in conversation and think about the dynamic interactions that connect them. One can start with adjacent systems, or one might set students to generate hypotheses about the proximal interactions of two non-adjacent systems. More advanced students may start with blank templates and generate a map of system interactions independently or in groups.

The first students who tested this model were excited to work out the connections they discovered.[47] But my favourite class sceptic wondered if Shakespeare 'really' cared about Corn. We embarked on research and enjoyed surprising (to us) results. First, in 1596, Queen Elizabeth levied two Proclamations that aimed to stabilise corn prices and redistribute grain to regions suffering a 'dearth'. In this context, 'corn' refers to any kind of grain (*OED*, corn, n.1). The second vehemently proclaims against those 'Badgers' who had created a black market for corn. To those who withheld their stock to create increased demand and raise prices, she dictated that they should be 'seuerly punished, to the terrour of others' (Elizabeth I, 1596). But the Crown struggled to enforce these proclamations throughout the country. In fact, Shakespeare appears to have been one of these 'Badgers'; he was prosecuted in February 1598 for retaining eighty bushels of corn during a food shortage (Archer et al., 2015: 10).

Although 'corn' in the period is often synonymous with grains like wheat, rye and barley, the repetition of 'maze' in Titania's speech cues us to

---

[46] See Appendix I for a downloadable blank template.

[47] This group comprised first-year undergraduates in a general education course.

think about its homonym *maize*, native to the Americas. Sir Walter Raleigh brought maize from America to England along with tobacco and potatoes in 1586; his cousin Sir Richard Grenville returned from a voyage with an Algonquin man from Roanoke whom he named 'Raleigh' (Watkins, 1792: 56–57). When we started thinking about the interacting systems that comprise the 'mazèd world' within and beyond the play, we did not expect to encounter evidence that exposes Shakespeare's questionable ethics, or that engaged *A Midsummer Night's Dream* in a vivid conversation with the Columbian Exchange.

More questions emerged. Does this play recast the theatre of the world as its near analogue in *contemptus mundi* – a metaphor that magnifies mediaeval Christian imperatives to hold worldliness in contempt?[48] Enno Ruge sees sixteenth-century Calvinists adopting the *contemptus mundi* topos to place themselves 'above' the spectacles in the theatre of the world (2014: 32). How might this 'contempt' for the 'world' function as a rationale for colonial exploitation? Or, from a presentist perspective, how might this contempt play out in debates surrounding climate change?

A Midsummer Night's Dream dramatises how diverse cosmological ecosystems interact across space and time. By exploring the play from non-human perspectives, one may see how 'worlds' might respond to their inhabitants' contempt. This repositioning of focal entities can help students sustain lines of inquiry from radically unfamiliar and frequently marginalised perspectives. Perhaps the most exciting element students can take away from *A Midsummer Night's Dream* is that it 'opens at the close' (Rowling, 2007: 134). That is to say, the close of one world-narrative opens another; every exit is an entrance to another place.[49] Shakespeare continues in this vein of possibility in *Henry V*, a 'Cronicle History' that foregrounds the audience's imagination as they are instructed to 'entertain conjecture of a time / when creeping murmur and the poring dark / fills the wide vessel of the universe' (Shakespeare, 2024g: 4.0.Sp1).

---

[48] See Greene (2020: 146).   [49] Cf. *AYLI*, Shakespeare, 2024b: 2.7.146–150.

'Conjecture of a Time': Henry V

The Prologue-like Chorus (hereafter Prologue) of *The Cronicle History of Henry V* subverts vertical power hierarchies as it swivels perspectives from the *theatrum mundi* to the play's performance space. The play's overt metatheatricality creates layers of performance that beg questions about conventional understandings of the theatre of the world metaphor, especially its associations with mediaeval conceptions of the body politic and the divine right of kings.[50] Consider the Prologue's repeated similes and allusion to acting:

> A kingdom for a stage, princes to act,
> And monarchs to behold the swelling scene.
> Then should the warlike Harry, like himself,
> Assume the port of Mars   (Pro.Sp.1)[51]

Repetition lends an epic tone to 'Harry's' (King Henry V's) apotheosis, his metamorphosis into the god of war. Yet 'warlike' and 'like' together undercut the transformation; Harry is himself and is not. He plays the *part* of Mars. His cloak of assumed divinity is a disguise, indistinguishable from what he wears among his men the night before the battle at Agincourt (see 4.1). A tacit question arises: is his Christian apotheosis and accession to the English throne also an act? This section's Explorations are designed to help students interpret the competing voices in the play, first by using digital approaches to text-analysis, and then by analysing how Shakespeare augments his historical sources. Students are encouraged to think about how politics and theatre engage in conversation.

Henry V was composed and performed while England was at war on multiple fronts. Between 1585 and 1604, Queen Elizabeth's privy council

---

[50] Metatheatre is a twentieth-century term that describes inter-theatrical stage practices that highlight the fictional layers within a play or a performance. See also Dustagheer and Newman (2018).

[51] Unless otherwise indicated, citations to *Henry V* hereafter follow Shakespeare, eds. J. Mardock and are given by act, scene, and speech.

authorised the deployment of roughly 6,500 men per year, some to fight Spain in the Low Countries, others to colonise Ireland (Cahill, 2008: 13). Patricia Cahill notes that 'virtually all able-bodied men who were not clergy and who were below the rank of baron and between the age of 16 and 60 were liable by statute for military service'. But in practice, it was the lower classes, 'the poor, the old, and the unwell' who were forced to serve Queen and country (Cahill, 2008: 14).[52] Students might reflect upon the demographics that comprise the military in their countries and how they are deployed. How would they feel if the draft were reinstated for all genders? Many have approached this play as an aspirational history that glorifies King Henry's French victories. But such interpretations require one to ignore the epilogue's reminder that monarchs die, and that hard-won lands are easily lost.

When the Prologue introduces 'this scaffold' as a synonym for the stage in *Henry V*, students can consider how it evokes the battles and casualties described both onstage and in the context of then-topical historical events. The Prologue's request that audiences 'judge' this play also raises the spectre of punishment: 'this scaffold' could be a platform for the hanging, disembowelment and execution of criminals. As James Mardock observes, this association with public spaces where classes mix invites speculation by commoners, 'while also suggesting that such speculation is itself transgressive' (in Lyly, 2025: para 2). As a pre-reading activity, students can create a rubric from which they may later assess Henry's performance. What qualities does one value in a leader? They may compare their criteria with those on offer in Shakespeare's sources, Edward Hall's 1548 chronicles (see Para 5) and Raphael Holinshed's later augmentations (2025). Should this play be judged in the context of the socio-cultural and political norms of mediaeval Europe? Those of Elizabethan England? Or, those of the twenty-first century?

Kristin M.S. Bezio recognises that leadership scholars generally have focussed on Henry's positive attributes, his 'rhetorical skill, personal accountability, self-confidence and affinity with the common man' (2013: 45). But, she suggests, they fail to recognise 'Shakespeare's awareness of the intricacies of leadership' (2013: 45). Bezio sees Henry engaged with *performing* leadership

---

[52] For more about mustering troops at this time, see Shapiro (2005: 64).

according to the moment he finds himself in. These performances suggest he is 'a flawed king who nevertheless is able to achieve success because he does not rely on a presumption of absolute authority' (Bezio, 2013: 54). Instead of ruling tyrannically, one finds Henry consulting others before making decisions, including his bishops, his soldiers, the French king and Catherine.[53] Inviting students to take the foregoing considerations into account may help them push past simplistic binaries as to whether Henry is a 'good' or 'bad' king and realise the complex dynamics that inform leadership – especially when one is responsible for the health of a diverse body politic.

Whereas a Chorus might conventionally set out the arguments that follow in the drama itself, that is not what happens here. Instead, as James Shapiro suggests, Shakespeare makes 'the alternation of the Chorus and the action rather than the rivalry of King Henry and the French Dauphin the main source of conflict' (2005: 301). Before each act, they insistently juxtapose rhetorical questions with mandates that audience members supplement stage-business with their imaginations: 'And let us, ciphers to this great account, / On your imaginary forces work' (Pro.Sp1).[54] They flatter, cajole and demand complicity as they ask audiences to adjudicate Henry's justification for war and treatment of his subjects. Meanwhile, they lead audiences through labyrinthine timescapes: 'now', 'here', 'there', 'o'er times', 'many years', 'hourglass' and 'history':

> For 'tis your thoughts that now must deck our kings,
> Carry them here and there, jumping o'er times,
> Turning th'accomplishment of many years
> Into an hourglass: for the which supply,
> Admit me Chorus to this history,
> Who, prologue-like, your humble patience pray
> Gently to hear, kindly to judge our play.   (Pro.Sp1)

---

[53] I follow Mardock's spelling of Catherine's name except when using the Folger Shakespeare edition for text analysis (Shakespeare, 2024g).

[54] Although early editors gender the Chorus male, likely due to the fact that female actors did not regularly take the stage until the seventeenth century, I have chosen they/them pronouns to recognise the role's gender fluidity.

Not only is 'the labour of imagination' thrust upon the audience, but so too judgement (Degenhardt, 2022: 200). Douglas Bruster and Robert Weimann claim that 'this demand for the audience to 'deck' royalty points to the need for an act of cooperation; such an act sanctions a medium of perception hitherto unauthorised in the popular theatre' (2004: 125). The phrase 'kindly to judge our play' may be an overused modesty trope but judgement is precisely what this Prologue sanctions. The question arises: Which monarch are audiences to judge?

Chronological distortions jump 'o'er times' to implicate both 'Harry' and the sitting monarch 'now'. Should audiences judge Harry's or the King's actions in the context of twelfth-century history, or Queen Elizabeth's in Shakespeare's time? Those interested in textual transmission history can compare the 1600 quarto that omits the Choral roles with the 1623 Folio edition; both are readily available online.[55] Without the Chorus figures, audiences may simply slip into the past and enjoy this historical narrative. But these figures repeatedly turn this theatrical mirror upon spectators and demand their presence *in* the present.

EXPLORATION: ADMIT ME CHORUS

This activity introduces students to distant reading practises using *Voyant-Tools*, an open-source text analysis platform with a short learning curve.[56] Distant reading allows one to use computational tools to analyse vast amounts of text in a non-linear fashion. The first step in text analysis is simply to count words; *Voyant-Tools* will do that for you. Its default settings include a list of what are called 'stop words'. These include function words like 'the', 'to' and 'of' as well as numbers and symbols. The programming has been designed to 'stop' counting these 'words' so users can focus on 'contentful' words (Froehlich, 2019: np).

---

[55] See: https://lemdo.uvic.ca/peer-review/emdH5_edition.html.
[56] Heather Froelich's essay 'Moby Dick is about whales, or why should we count words?' offers students an accessible introduction to using distant reading methods to complement conventional close reading practices (2019). For help getting started using the Voyant platform, see 'Guides: Voyant Tools Help', https://voyant-tools.org/docs/#!/guide.

EXPLORATION (cont.)

Getting Started

Upon uploading document(s), one may choose to work with an array of visualisations from the basic word cloud, trends, summary and words-in-context features, to a growing list of more sophisticated and evolving outputs.[57]

The following example models how one might analyse the data provided in the 'Summary' pane. Here, I used the Folger Shakespeare's API (Application Program Interface) to create three documents for analysis (https://www.folgerdigitaltexts.org/api). To extract these selections, I first selected 'Text by character' and chose the 'Chorus'; this option gave me the Chorus' lines from its 'Prologue-like' introduction through the epilogue; I used the same feature to extract King Henry's lines. Next, I selected 'Text, minus a character's' and again chose the Chorus, this time to remove their lines. I created three documents, respectively entitled: HV-Chorus, HV-Henry and HV-SansChorus ('sans' = without).[58] Next, I uploaded all three extracts into Voyant-tools for comparison. I was curious to see whether there might be any statistical differences in the words used by the Chorus and those in the body of the play (Figure 8).

Question and Reflect

Once you create a visualisation, the next step is to make observations and ask questions. In this case, it may be surprising that the Chorus'

---

[57] Jonathan Hope's 'Digital Approaches to Shakespeare's Language' provides additional suggestions and tools for teaching introductory text-analysis in the classroom (2019).

[58] One should give files short and recognisable names to facilitate analysis in the visualisation panes.

EXPLORATION (cont.)

vocabulary density is nearly *triple* that of the play-text alone.[59] Vocabulary density measures the use and repetition of contentful words. The longer sentences and higher readability index scores numerically confirm that the Chorus' language is significantly more complex than the rest of the play. Why are the styles of these two bodies of text so dramatically different? Students might observe that in the top ten distinctive words of the Chorus commands are prominent: 'behold' (9) and 'suppose' (2). How many imperative (command) verbs can they identify in the first Chorus? What are they (e.g. let, suppose, piece, divide, make, think, carry, jump, admit, hear, judge)? Additionally, students can compare the differences among distinctive words between the Chorus and the body-text. What themes emerge? If 'France' is a focal theme, then why does the Chorus alone redirect audiences to 'London' repeatedly? Ask students how language 'works' on them as the Chorus will later urge: 'Work, work your thoughts' (3.0.Sp1).

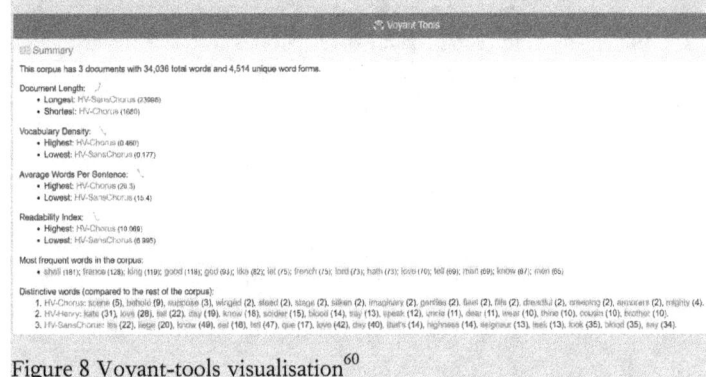

Figure 8 Voyant-tools visualisation[60]

---

[59] HV-Chorus's vocabulary density is .460 compared to HV-SansChorus's .177.

[60] *Voyant Tools*, Summary, Created 29 October 2023, https://voyant-tools.org/?corpus=26a47964e5c145867a7ed888c182fe44&view=Summary.

> EXPLORATION (cont.)
>
> Finally, the most frequent distinctive words from the lines spoken by King Henry are surprising: 'Kate' and 'love'.[61] Although Catherine of France and her nurse share a wonderful scene wherein she practises translating the names of body parts from French into English, only King Henry calls her 'Kate' and only in the final act of the play.[62] What might this repetition in conjunction with 'love' suggest? Is this romantic? Or, is it a form of linguistic coercion? Students and teachers might recreate these or other corpora and play more with Voyant-tools to see what other patterns may emerge.[63] One might select scenes featuring the King and compare them with scenes where his soldiers from various regions take the stage. Or, one might dive deeply into topic-generated terminology surrounding justice, monarchy, bodies or love. Teachers can create a shared document to collect visualisations, hypotheses and questions that can help students identify emerging patterns of thought.

These competing bodies of text formally draw attention to the play's anatomisation of the 'body politic', a mediaeval microcosm of the theatre of the world. Before I gloss this metaphor, one should recall that Shakespeare's audiences likely would have been familiar with Prince Hal's (Henry V's nickname in the *I Henry IV* plays) early life as a wild child cavorting with Sir John Falstaff, Pistol, Bardolph, Nym and the Hostess from the two *Henry IV* plays. In Act 1, Canterbury describes the prince's transformation upon his father's death:

---

[61] The Folger eds. of *Henry V* most suitable for text analysis spell Catherine's name with 'K' (Shakespeare, 2024g).

[62] For an excellent discussion of Catherine's role in the body politic, see Waldron (2022).

[63] See 'The Four Points of Character Analysis' for information about using the Folger Shakespeare's API to create corpora by character and more in Section 1.

> The courses of his youth promised it not.
> The breath no sooner left his father's body,
> But that his wildness, mortified in him,
> Seemed to die too. Yea, at that very moment,
> Consideration like an angel came,
> And whipped th'offending Adam out of him,
> Leaving his body as a paradise,
> T'envelop and contain celestial spirits. (1.1.Sp9)

Anyone who has lost a parent has been transformed by the experience, but what Canterbury describes is supernatural. Not only is the King's wildness exorcised, but so too is the 'offending Adam' and its associations with mortal bodies. According to the divine right of kings, Henry's inheritance of the throne transforms him into a container for 'celestial spirits', the Christian God's representative on earth. In this play, however, the Chorus figures remain sceptical about this transformation. Never do they refer to the King as 'Henry', but always 'Harry', a diminutive that indicates familiarity yet undercuts divinity. He may no longer be the wild 'Prince Hal' but from the Chorus' perspective, nor is he an embodiment of God's will.

These two sides of Henry/Harry, combined with the competing bodies of text, engage what Ernst Kantorowicz describes as the 'two bodies' metaphor. This concept, first documented in Edmund Plowden's *Reports*, arose from a legal debate over a lease made by the underage Edward IV. To protect royal interests, Queen Elizabeth's lawyers invented the idea of the 'King's Two Bodies', distinguishing between the king's natural body and his political body. The political body, unlike the natural body, is immune to physical defects and age, ensuring that actions taken in the king's political capacity remain valid despite any limitations of his natural body (Kantorowicz, 1957: 7). This duality challenges Elizabethan jurists to maintain both the unity and separation of these two bodies. Students can consider how Shakespeare's linguistic representation of the play's 'two bodies' supports or undercuts this metaphor.

Henry V thematically and formally puts pressure on 'the body politic' as a philosophical 'proof' that supports the divine right of kings and its vertical class hierarchies. This concept ties the well-being of a state directly to the orderly workings of its metaphorical head, arms, stomach, legs and feet. Christine de Pizan, a contemporary of the historical King Henry, emphasises these class hierarchies. According to de Pizan, 'below' the monarch, knights and nobles: 'the other, common, people are like the stomach, feet and legs. For just as the stomach receives things procured by the head and the limbs, the deeds of princes and nobles will be for the good and love of the public; and just as the legs and feet support the actions of the human body, similarly the workers support all the other estates' (1997: 203).[64] Following John of Salisbury, de Pizan positions the torso, legs and feet as a capacious socio-cultural 'other', a subservient caste without social mobility or clear lines of communication to its head.[65] When John describes the 'feet' of the republic, he does not sustain metaphorical humanity: 'the number of feet in the republic surpasses not only the eight-footed crab, but even the centipede; one cannot enumerate them'. Although 'inferiors must serve superiors', John also maintains the opposite. The republic must keep their metaphorical feet in 'shoes'. John concludes that 'an afflicted people is like proof and irrefutable demonstration of the prince's gout' (1990: VI.20.126). Gout is a disease brought on by over-indulgence in luxury foods and alcohol; it tends to manifest in foot pain and swelling.

John does not continue here to suggest that diseased 'feet' might lead to rebellion against the 'head' of the body politic. But Shakespeare's Chorus appears to do just that:

> O England, model to thy inward greatness,
> Like little body with a mighty heart,
> What mightst thou do, that honour would thee do,
> Were all thy children kind and natural! (2.0.Sp1)

Here, the problem is that England's 'body' has produced 'children' who are neither 'kind' nor 'natural'. On one level of interpretation, the Chorus sets

---

[64] Blumenfeld cites John of Salisbury's *Policraticus* for de Pizan's primary source here (1997: 202).

[65] See Rollo-Koster (2017) for a discussion of 'caste' in the context of the body politic.

the stage for the revelation and execution of the English traitors who conspired with the French to plot the King's death. On another level, Henry is also a child of England's body politic. Might the Chorus suggest that his person is somehow unkind or unnatural?

This moment is framed by two scenes in which the King has betrayed John Falstaff, his ostensible father figure in Shakespeare's *Henry IV* plays. Act 2.1 recalls scenes from these plays, specifically 'Prince Hal's' friendships with Falstaff, Bardolph, Nym, Pistol and the Hostess. When the Boy enters to tell them that Falstaff is seriously ill, the Hostess diagnoses his disease: 'The King has killed his heart' (2.1.Sp.26). Nym and Pistol also find the king responsible for Falstaff's illness (2.1.Sp41-Sp42). When Henry became king, he turned his back on his close companion. Canterbury read this act as indicative of Henry's divinity, yet his former friends see it as a betrayal.

Act 2.2 shifts to reveal the titled traitors in King Henry's midst and his decision to execute them. 'The mercy that was quick in us' has dissolved. The King's long speech reveals these betrayals as not only political but also personal. He bore Cambridge 'love', and Scroop 'knews't the very bottom of [his] soul' (2.2.Sp25). 'Touching our person', Henry claims, 'we seek no revenge. But we our kingdom's safety must so tender' (2.2.Sp30). This may sound big of him, but the placement of this scene combined with their summary execution is suspect. The very next scene reveals Falstaff has died. Turning his back on his friends when he becomes king not only signals Henry's dubious character, but also can raise questions about his leadership. As head of England's body politic, Henry is responsible for his metaphorical appendages. Or, in the context of Canterbury's apiary metaphor, his 'drones' (cf. 1.2.Sp21). The Hostess's address to her 'honey-sweet husband' situates Henry's former companions in this essential yet paradoxically expendable class of English subjects.

Henry V's anatomies of the body politic put pressure on the viability of a divine monarchy as a post-mediaeval political model. This play's investment in anatomising the monarch's role in the theatre of the world is underscored by Shakespeare's generous augmentation of his sources. The following activity invites students to analyse how Shakespeare adapts and builds upon his sources to develop concepts which raise questions about leadership that remain not merely relevant, but urgent.

EXPLORATION: SHAKESPEARE'S SOURCES

Gillian Woods and Laura Seymour have rightly observed that random source study is hardly helpful, so I have provided direction to help students analyse the effect of Shakespeare's omissions and augmentations in the play (2019: 227). The pairings below provide opportunities to help students discover not simply shared points of contact, but also differences in tone, arrangement and conceptual development.

Getting Started

The following are excerpts from historical and philosophical works that Shakespeare likely consulted as he developed his own ideas about the body politic. Catherine's character is not developed in the sources; her scenes are the playwright's invention. Here too, students are invited to consider the play's epilogue, to contemplate some themes surrounding this *topos*, as well as its associations with the divine right of kings and succession. Ask students to consider what Shakespeare retains and omits from his sources as they analyse these excerpts to develop their understanding of the body politic and the historical contexts from which the play was partially drawn.

The Body Politic

1. Exeter: 1.2.Sp20

    Compare with sources:

    Hall (2025: Para 26; Para 20)

    John of Salisbury, *Policraticus* (1990: Book VI, Chs. 20–21, 125–127)

2. Canterbury: 1.2.Sp21

    Compare with John (1990: Ch. 21)

3. Catherine and Alice: 3.4; Catherine and Henry: 5.2

    These scenes are *not* in Shakespeare's sources. How do these additions develop the concept of the body politic?

> ### EXPLORATION (cont.)
>
> Historical Episodes
>
> > Source texts: Hall (2025); Holinshed (2025)
> > 1. 'The Tennis Ball Embassy'
> >   Compare with sources:
> >   > Hall (Para 35); Holinshed (Para 13)
> >   > Shakespeare (1.2.Sp25-30)
> >
> > 2. 'The Southampton Treason'
> >   Compare with sources:
> >   > Holinshed (Para 30-33)
> >   > Shakespeare (2.2)
> >
> > 3. Before the Battle of Agincourt
> >   Compare with sources:
> >   > Hall (Para 36–45); Holinshed (Para 58)
> >   > Shakespeare (4.3.Sp10)
>
> ### Question and Reflect
>
> As students compare and contrast Shakespeare's play with its sources, they should ask: What does Shakespeare keep? What does he omit? How do tone and sentiment change from history to play? Both sections offer occasions for students to generate hypotheses and raise additional questions for class discussion.

France was won and lost between the end of Act 5 and the Epilogue. The rival perspectives dramatised throughout *Henry V* draw attention to competing belief systems and raise questions about how justice is and should be adjudicated in times of change. Linear hierarchies and historical precedents surrounding the divine right of kings and their succession are simultaneously glorified and undercut. The play's hyper-theatricality and enactment of plural world-systems of the Chorus and the playtext situate the King as an actor in the theatre of the world. As such, he will be judged both by God and by history. One wonders at the concurrence of the 1599 Bishop's Ban on all history plays and performances of *Henry V* (See Section 2). To my mind, this play's sceptical treatment of historical precedents clearly posed a threat to those protecting Queen Elizabeth's position, not least because her reign was assured not by divine law, but by her father King Henry VIII's will. Despite Hollywood and stage directors who insist this play enacts an epitome of patriotic glory, students might reflect upon what directors have had to cut to achieve that effect.

Just as the formal differences between the Chorus and play-text provide a parallax framework from which to compare competing versions of world order, so do the chronological microcosms that constitute each act and scene. As I discussed in Section 1, parallax provides a frame for thinking from two perspectives to discover a third. One finds Shakespeare continuing to experiment with these formal structures in *Hamlet*. In addition to the play's transparent metatheatricality, Hamlet's soliloquies similarly contrast with the action of the play-text to create multiple world-systems and to interrogate the relation of one's inner world to those it interacts with.

'This Distracted Globe': Hamlet

Hamlet's famous 'To be or not to be' soliloquy raises complex questions about what it means to be an actor in the 'theatre of the world' (Shakespeare, 2006a: 3.1.55–88). One challenge is, much as we saw in *Othello*, that 'seeming' and 'being' are often at odds and defy clear distinctions. Hamlet's soliloquy meditates how one should act in the 'play' of life as he wonders at his role beyond in the *theatrum mundi*. The 'to be' speech is marvellously provocative because it queries the role of the individual across different planes of 'being'. Similarly, Hamlet's 'distracted globe' emerges as a scalar device that challenges understanding one's role on a world stage that emerges from relative perspectives.

This subsection's Explorations ask students to hold two or more perspectives in mind and to consider what additional viewpoints emerge. The first provides a close reading exercise that recalls earlier discussions of parallax and introduces students to the literary figure 'hendiadys' in the context of the play's textual variants. The second introduces accessible approaches to recognising the play's metatheatrical elements, notably the play-within-a-play, that are scalable for different skill levels. If 'all the world's a stage, and all the men and women merely players' (Shakespeare, 2024b: 2.7.146), then *Hamlet* finds Shakespeare querying the reaches of an actor's apprehension of world-systems in what he calls: 'this distracted globe' (Shakespeare, Q2, 2024e: 782).

'Distracted' describes the senses of disintegration, dissolution and division that are consistent with Shakespeare's sustained reflections on the untethering of terrestrial and cosmographical systems from ancient models (*OED*, distracted, v. and adj.). The play-text of *Hamlet* is also distracted, circulating in sundry variants. Printed in 1603, the first quarto (hereafter Q1) is believed to be a memorial reconstruction of the play, likely from the perspective of the actor Marcellus (Wells and Taylor, rpt. 1997: 398; Thompson and Taylor 2006a: 12).[66] This edition is shorter than and quite different from its successors; Zachary Lesser's *Hamlet After Q1* (2015) details the nineteenth-century discovery of Q1 and its reception history. *Hamlet* was published again in 1604 (Q2). Q2 is longer and more polished than Q1, more closely resembling today's popular editions.[67] Exploring *Hamlet's* textual history can help students engage with the play's dramatisation of shifting perspectives that generate diverse epistemologies, or ways of knowing, for actors in the theatre of the world.

---

[66] 'Quarto' describes how a playbook is made, specifically by folding leaves into four quadrants. Shakespeare's early quartos are more like pamphlets than 'books', as they were rarely bound. A 'folio' describes a book made by folding the paper in two; Shakespeare's 'First Folio' was constructed this way. For an accessible guide to early bookmaking, see Egan (2010: 231–236).

[67] See also *PBS Hamlet, Shakespeare Uncovered* (2013) featuring David Tennant discussing the play-text's history, https://archive.org/details/pbs-hamlet-shakespeare-uncovered.

The following Exploration invites students to practise close reading as they pay special attention to the workings of a rhetorical form of parallax called *hendiadys*. Hendiadys describes how meaning emerges from the combination of two words: 'O, 'tis most sweet / When in one line two crafts directly meet' (Shakespeare, 2024e: 2576–2577).[68] Both Frank Kermode (2000: 101–102), and from a different perspective, Robert N. Watson, have discussed how Shakespeare employs hendiadys to generate novel linguistic combinations, whether for the sake of art or entertainment (2014: 86–106). Here, parallax provides a framework that may help students reflect how two perspectives can combine to produce novel third terms. Slavoj Žižek's arguments for dialectical materialism may be of interest to advanced students, but even beginners might appreciate his challenge to tidy approaches to semantic parallax (2006: 4). If one approaches what Žižek calls the 'parallax gap' in a figure of paired words and/or concepts, one may discover Shakespeare subverting convention to again recall Touchstone and contemplate the virtue in 'if' (*As You Like It*, 2024b: 5.4.106–107). Some students may be tempted to ignore this linguistic doubling and get to a 'point' (Shakespeare, *Ham.*, [1603] 2006: 7.115), but what if 'one line' of inquiry is not Shakespeare's aim in his insistent appositions of similar-but-different words?

EXPLORATION: PARALLAX AND HENDIADYS

The following excerpts are from Internet Shakespeare Editions (ISE), an open-source publication where one can find variant editions with both original and modern spelling. The driving question is: How do differences across editions generate alternate suggestions about personal agency in the *theatrum mundi*? Students can use the *OED* or another favourite dictionary to carefully analyse each sentence.

---

[68] Citations to *Hamlet* are given across several editions as indicated. The Internet Shakespeare Editions of Q1 (Shakespeare, 2024d), Q2 (Shakespeare, 2024e), and F1 (2024f) provide throughline numbers instead of acts and scenes.

EXPLORATION (cont.)

Getting Started

Students can first explore the hendiadys that emerge in 'grieu'd and sallied'. How do the several connotations of 'grieu'd' (including 'aggrieved') and 'sallied' interact? These two words are similar but different: what senses emerge from their specific arrangement? How do these different senses inform this 'sentence' – in relation to both the series of words and the thought conveyed (*OED*, 'sentence', n.)?

> O that this too much grieu'd and sallied flesh
> Would melt to nothing, or that the vniuersall
> Globe of heauen would turne al to a Chaos!
> (Shakespeare, 2024d: 311–313.1)

Question and Reflect

Etymologies here reveal opportunities for complex interpretations. 'Grieu'd' may indicate sadness, but it also suggests physical violence and literal damage (*OED*, grieve, v. 2, 3). 'Sallied' is associated with an eruption of martial force, a burst of elements followed by their dispersal (*OED*, sally, v.1). Although some editors later emend this word to 'solid', students might productively brainstorm with different connotations. Why might Shakespeare frame Hamlet's state of mind with these two similar-but-different words? What kinds of third terms emerge through parallax?

The following two excerpts reflect textual emendations that were respectively made in 1604 and 1623. Neither features formal hendiadys, but students can still continue close-reading linguistic similarities and differences. Does repetition function like a synonym, or something else? Ask students to analyse how even slight shifts in a word's connotations can alter one's perspective and understanding.

> ### EXPLORATION (cont.)
>
> Oh, that this too too sallied flesh would melt,
> Thaw, and resolve itself into a dew! (Shakespeare, 2024e: 312–313)
> Oh that this too too solid Flesh, would melt,
> Thaw, and resolue it selfe into a Dew (Shakespeare, 2024f: 312–313)
>
> The foregoing excerpts also beg questions about how editors inform one's reception of Shakespeare's works. For example, let's look at individual word choices across the three editions under discussion:
>
> > Grieu'd and sallied (Q1)
> > Too too sallied (Q2)
> > Too too solid (Q3)
>
> Although George T. Wright's list of sixty-six hendiadys found in *Hamlet* does not include 'grieu'd and sallied' because they are from Q1, the doubling of adjectives that describe injury and dispersal underscore the dissolution of flesh that the more metrical 'too too' emphasises in Q2 (1981: 185–188).[69] Here, one may also recognise how 'Shakespeare' is constructed and reconstructed from moving parts, notably combinations of variant editions not limited to those published during his lifetime. For example, the First Folio arguably has informed centuries of understandings surrounding Shakespeare's role in 'this distracted globe' (Shakespeare, 2024e: 782).[70]

Hamlet's 'distracted globe' manifests multiple connotations that collide across vastly different scales of relation:

> O all you host of heaven! O earth! What else?
> And shall I couple hell? Oh, fie! Hold, hold, my heart,

---

[69] Wright's lists are extensive; teachers may choose to focus on any of the many instances of these figurative repetitions in *Hamlet*.

[70] Much has been written about F1 in the wake of its 400th anniversary. See especially Emma Smith's *Shakespeare's First Folio* (2016, rpt. 2023).

> And you, my sinews, grow not instant old,
> But bear me swiftly up. Remember thee?
> Ay, thou poor ghost, whiles memory holds a seat
> In this distracted globe. Remember thee?
>
> (Shakespeare, 2024e: 787–802)

'Globe' emerges here as a scalar device that simultaneously juxtaposes the macrocosm containing interacting systems that include heaven, earth and hell with Hamlet's heart, sinews and skull: the container of his memory. 'All you' underscores plurality. Students can consider how Hamlet's 'globe' is a metonymy for key themes in the play, not limited to 'remembering', but extending to cognition, conscience and cosmology.

This 'distracted globe' carries with it a 'coincidence of multiple globes' that invite reflection upon its scalar connotations (Goldberg et al., 2016: 11). Gavin Hollis's extension of Craig Dionne's conception of the 'sphere reflex' is helpful here. One finds characters negotiating 'views from above and from below' in 'global' or 'spherical' terms: 'they think with a small object – say an egg or a shell – in order to explain a larger phenomenon . . . or with a large object – say, a celestial body – to explain a more localised phenomenon . . . Thinking spherically becomes a gesture toward the comprehension of their world' (Hollis, 2022: 248). The foregoing passage demonstrates Hamlet engaged in precisely this kind of cognitive activity as he tries to make sense of a universal 'globe' that paradoxically contains and looses heaven, earth, hell and a supernatural realm of ghosts.

Simultaneously, 'this distracted globe' links the 'world of the mind' to Shakespeare's eponymous 'Globe' theatre (Goldberg et al., 2016: 11). How does Hamlet's 'seat' of memory, or 'distracted globe' extend from the Globe theatre in which the play might be performed to the theatre of the world? Do these multiple 'globes' collide randomly throughout the universe, or are they part of a macrocosmic whole?[71] Teachers might ask students to deliberate how 'globe' functions as what Roland Greene has called an 'engine-word' (2020:

---

[71] Students can consider these questions also in the context of the title page and prefatory sonnet ('The Minde of the Front') in *The History of the World* by Sir Walter Raleigh (1614).

163), and replace 'world' with 'globe' in the 'What is a world?' Exploration in Section 1.

Hamlet's 'distracted globe' emphasises these associations of separation and totality through the play's metatheatrical elements. Metatheatre, a term coined in the twentieth century, broadly refers to how plays highlight their own artificial nature through devices like the play-within-a-play.[72] In classroom settings, some of these discussions often get bogged down in overly detailed arguments that can be confusing. However, Stephen Purcell's suggestion that Shakespearean metatheatricality operates similarly to a pun can help students recognise how metatheatre yokes different narrative planes together. Puns bring two distinct ideas into collision, relying on the reader's ability to simultaneously recognise the coexistence of these ideas within the same utterance (2018: 22). Purcell offers 'a good pun is its own re-word' as an example that recombines the cliché 'virtue is its own reward' with 're-wording', or linguistic facility (2018: 22). How many interpretations can students generate from the collision of 'virtue' and 'words'? Parallax again provides a frame to think about what emerges from the gap between two separate ideas. One can apply a similar approach to interpreting the metatheatrical elements of Shakespeare's plays.

In Hamlet, the famous line 'the play's the thing' underscores the significance of theatrical performance, and the play-within-a-play draws attention to the tension between verisimilitude and artifice (Shakespeare, 2024d: 1644). This metatheatrical device creates a mirroring effect by staging a microcosm of the play's central themes. Through this dramatic reflection, the audience is invited to scrutinize the characters' performances. Within the satirical framework of the *theatrum mundi*, this mirroring aims to expose the hypocrisies of individuals, groups and governments, both among the actors onstage and the spectators observing them. Hamlet expresses this concept when he reflects:

> I have heard
> That guilty creatures sitting at a play
> Have by the very cunning of the scene

---

[72] For a survey of contemporary criticism surrounding use of the term 'metatheatre' see Sarah Dustagheer and Harry Newman (2018: 3–18).

> Been struck so to the soul that presently
> They have proclaimed their malefactions
>
> (Shakespeare, 2006a: 2.2.523–527)

He thus hatches a plot to test the ghost's claim that Claudius murdered his father: 'the play's the thing / Wherein I'll catch the conscience of the King' (2006a: 2.2.539–540). By mirroring enactments of Claudius' supposed crime onstage, Hamlet hopes to find his guilt or innocence reflected in his stepfather's demeanour. One might ask students to imagine that they're watching a favourite show with friends that features a scene that mirrors something they have done that makes them feel guilty or shameful. Would they fidget or laugh nervously? Might their face betray discomfort? With their responses in mind, do they think Hamlet's strategy will work?

EXPLORATION: METATHEATRE

The following activity invites students to put metatheatrical elements of *Hamlet* into collision. Much like the last Exploration, the goal is to explore how two or more concepts combine to produce interpretations that contribute depth and texture to their understandings of the play. This activity aims to help students recognise these metatheatrical components as interacting play-worlds that generate meaning from shared points of contact. Beginning students might focus on Part One, whereas more advanced students might combine Parts One and Two.

Getting Started

Part One: Identifying Play-Worlds

1. Identification: Begin by directing students to identify the distinct play-worlds staged within the Danish court. Encourage them to start

EXPLORATION (cont.)

with the dumb show (a silent performance) and 'The Murder of Gonzago', which Hamlet also refers to as 'The Mousetrap'.

2. Character Analysis: Discuss how these staged mirror-figures for Hamlet Sr., Claudius and Gertrude inform our understanding of their motivations. For instance, Ophelia's observation, 'The lady doth protest too much, methinks' (2006: 3.2.224), can be compared with Hamlet's insistence that the play is not topical but originates in Italy (2006: 3.2.254–257).
3. Reflection: Ask students to reflect on the individual play-worlds before considering how Ophelia's, Hamlet's and Claudius' narrative interjections create points of collision. Discuss what emerges from these collisions and how they impact the overall narrative.

Part Two: Comparing Variants

1. Textual Analysis: Compare early variants of these scenes, focusing on changes between Q1 (1603) and later editions. Analyse how these changes affect the portrayal of individual characters and their motivations.
2. Impact on Interpretation: Ask students to consider how slight changes in the representations of the dumb show and 'The Mousetrap' (The Murder of Gonzago), as well as the points of collision between these play-worlds and Hamlet, influence their interpretation of the play as a whole.

Question and Reflect

How might Hamlet's conflation of *The Mousetrap* and its source text speak to strategies Shakespeare himself uses across his corpus? Here one might revisit *Othello's* adaptation of Cinthio, or *Henry V's* blending of history and fiction. What effects arise from recombining narrative microcosms? How might these effects relate to themes and concepts discussed throughout this Element, such as constructions of identity,

> EXPLORATION (cont.)
>
> law and justice, the interplay between appearance and reality, enactments of the body politic, and the concept of the world as a stage?

Ultimately, *Hamlet* demonstrates that knowledge – of the macrocosmic globe and microcosmic human – is more relative than fixed. Similar to Debapriya Sarkar's claim about Sir Philip Sidney's *Defense of Poesy*, each play under discussion experiments with formal elements to envision 'a reality that could be otherwise, suggesting a literary epistemology that understands knowledge as conceivable rather than verifiable' (2023: 2). If, as Harold Bloom claims, *Hamlet* '*is* theatre of the world' (my emphasis, 1999: 383), then this rhetorical device emerges as a framework for testing and retesting characters' performances from the several perspectives afforded by shifting stages. In a classroom, these stages might be the paper ones of variant texts and editions, or they may be vivified in performance. *Hamlet* cannot be tidily resolved, but instead requires readers and audiences alike to consider ranging possibilities. Like the rest of the plays under discussion here, *Hamlet* provides an opportunity to help students develop habits of mind from which they regularly will consider all possibilities and test hypotheses from multiple perspectives.

Coda: Who's There?

> Touchstone: The more pity that fools may not speak wisely what wise
> men do foolishly.   (Shakespeare, 2024b: 1.2.83)

Each school term, I study my classroom roster before the first meeting and wonder: 'who's there?' Ten years ago, students' names would have given me a general idea of gender and heritage demographics. Now, however, these rosters are unhelpful. My students might present as part of one or another racial, gendered or neurological group, but identify in more ways than one. Most are teens and early twenty-somethings, so they are still working out who they are and who they want to be. Like Shakespeare, they must figure out how to make not just a living but a *life*, in a world where 'order' is hard to find.

'Who's there?' also has grown into an increasingly sinister question. Just as Shakespeare and his contemporaries had to be mindful of what they said and how they said it, so do we. In today's post-truth information climate, facts are frequently distorted, re-contextualised and re-deployed to support false narratives that have dire consequences. Given a global rise in academic censorship, it has become dangerous to voice opinion, let alone speak truth to power. In America, the government has launched an all-out attack on education, dismantling the Department of Education and cutting funding for academic research across disciplines. Although these actions have left many of us living in Western nations reeling from shock, for Shakespeare and his contemporaries, censorship was part of daily life.

Every play performed in Elizabethan London was first subject to approval by the Master of Revels. But censorship was not limited to public stages. Individuals were prosecuted for things they were *thought* to believe or know. For example, Thomas Kyd, author of *The Spanish Tragedy*, a blockbuster play that influenced Shakespeare's *Hamlet*, was arrested by the Crown and tortured until he provided 'information' about his flat-mate and playwright Christopher Marlowe. Kyd was not suspected of any real crime – Crown agents were after information. Still, he died from his treatment in prison shortly after his release from prison.[73]

That censorship, of course, influenced what could be said in both life and art. All socio-political and theological commentary had to make it past these government authorities. Therefore, Shakespeare's works rarely offer direct topical commentary. When students today encounter difficulties with Shakespeare's complexity, it can help to make these conditions of composition transparent. How might one speak truth to power when direct speech is punishable by law? Social media culture is so influential that it doesn't need

---

[73] For an excellent account of Kyd's relationship with Marlowe, see Nicholl (1994).

legal measures to penalise people for having opposing views. What impact has that had on how students construct their own beliefs?

By revisiting Shakespeare's works through the theatre of the world *topos*, one may find him developing diverse perspectives and raising questions about socio-political constructions of identity and justice that have, to my mind, never been more pressing. Third-year university student Tara Cormier reflects on their experience studying Shakespeare and his contemporaries: 'These plays aren't just stories; their very existence is an instruction manual for how to survive when it feels like the world is ending and you're powerless to stop it'. What is Shakespeare – what is literature – if not a portal to another world, insight into another time, a vehicle through which one may give and receive understanding, insight and empathy?

References

Abbeyelder (2022) A Figure Showing Bronfenbrenner's Ecological Theory. *Wikimedia Commons*, https://commons.wikimedia.org/wiki/File:Bronfenbrenner%27s_Ecological_Theory_of_Development.png.

Archer, J. E., Thomas, H. & Turley, R. M. (2015) Reading Shakespeare with the Grain: Sustainability and the Hunger Business. *Green Letters*, 19(1), 8–20.

Aristotle (2018) Poetics. Translated by S. H. Butcher. In J. E. Gainor, S. B. Garner Jr. & M. Puchner (eds.), *The Norton Anthology of Drama, Shorter 3rd ed*. New York: W.W. Norton, 135–150.

Baer, B. C. (2019) Snakes and Ladders. *Modernism/Modernity*, 3(4), np. https://doi.org/10.26597/mod.0091.

Baldwin, A. & Erickson, B. (2020) Introduction: Whiteness, coloniality, and the Anthropocene. *Environment and Planning D: Society and Space*, (38)1, 3–11.

Bate, J. (1998) *The Genius of Shakespeare*. New York: Oxford University Press.

Bennett, K. A. (2019) The API in Action: The Four Points of Character Analysis. The Folger Shakespeare API. www.folgerdigitaltexts.org/api.

Bennett, K. A. (2021) Digital Commonplace Books, *The Kit Marlowe Project*. https://kitmarlowe.org/digital_commonplace_book/5631/.

Bennett, K. A. (2022) Introduction to the Special Issue: Early Modern English Sati/yre. *Explorations on Renaissance Culture*, 48(1), 1–5.

Bennett, K. A. & Talamo, I. (2024) Theatre of the World (Media Group). *Folger Shakespeare Library*, https://digitalcollections.folger.edu/view/group/211754.

Bezio, K. M. S. (2013) Personating Leadership: Shakespeare's *Henry V* and Performative Negotiation. *Leadership and the Humanities*, 1(1), 43–58.

Bloom, H. (1999) *Shakespeare: The Invention of the Human*. New York: Riverhead Books.

Boaistuau, P. (1581) *Le Théâtre du Monde*. Translated by J. Alday. London: T. East for J. Wyght. STC 3170. Early English Books Online.

British Library. (2024) www.bl.uk/.

Britton, D. A. (2011) Re-'Turning' 'Othello': Transformative and Restorative Romance. *ELH*, 78(1), 27–50.

Britton, D. A. (2021) *Flesh and Blood: Race and Religion in The Merchant of Venice. The Cambridge Companion to Shakespeare and Race*. Edited by A. Thompson. Cambridge: Cambridge University Press, 108–122.

Bronfenbrenner, U. (1979) *The Ecology of Human Development: Experiments by Nature and Design*. Cambridge, MA: Harvard University Press.

Brown, D. S. (2023) *Shakespeare's White Others*. Cambridge: Cambridge University Press.

Brown, P. A. & Howard J. E. (eds.) (2014) *William Shakespeare, As You Like It: Texts and Contexts*. Boston: Bedford/St. Martin's.

Bruno, G. & Gatti, H. (2018) *The Ash Wednesday Supper: A New Translation*. Toronto: University of Toronto Press.

Bruster, D. & Weimann, R. (2004) *Prologues to Shakespeare's Theatre: Performance and Liminality in Early Modern Drama*. London: Routledge.

Burrow, J. A. (1986) *The Ages of Man: A Study in Medieval Writing and Thought*. Oxford: Clarendon Press.

Cahill, P. (2008) *Unto the Breach: Martial Formations, Historical Trauma, and the Early Modern Stage*. Oxford: Oxford University Press.

Campbell, M. (2023) *Behind the Name*. www.behindthename.com.

Cetera-Włodarczyk, A., Hope, J. & Włodarczyk, J. (2021) Unsphered, Disorbed, Decentred: Shakespeare's Astronomical Imagination. *Shakespeare*, 17(4), 400–427.

Chaucer, G. (2007) Parliament of Fowls. In K. L. Lynch (ed.), *Dream Visions and Other Poems*. New York: W.W. Norton, 93–116.

Cicero, M. T. (2000) *De Re Publica*. Translated by C. W. Keyes. Cambridge, MA: Harvard University Press, Loeb Classical Library.

Cinthio, G. (2000) *The Moor of Venice*. Translated by J. E. Taylor. Ontario: In Parentheses Publications, Medieval Italian Series, www.yorku.ca/inpar/cinthio_moor_taylor.pdf.

Clark, S. (2007) *Vanities of the Eye: Vision in Early Modern European Culture*. Oxford: Oxford University Press.

Clark, T. (2012) Derangements of Scale. In T. Cohen (ed.), *Telemorphosis: Theory in the Era of Climate Change*. Ann Arbor: University of Michigan. 148–166.

Colthorpe, M. E. (2017) Elizabethan Court Day by Day. *Folgerpedia*. https://folgerpedia.folger.edu/The_Elizabethan_Court_Day_by_Day.

Compagnoni, M. (2022) 'Speak of Me as [...]': Refashioning Geographies of Monstrosity in *Othello*. *Cahiers Élisabéthains: A Journal of English Renaissance Studies*, 108(1), 64–67.

Copeland, O. (2023) How to Add Alt-text in Google Slides. *The Kit Marlowe Project*, https://kitmarlowe.org/ho/7816/.

Cowart, J. (2017) *Earthrise – Apollo 8*. Wikimedia Commons, https://commons.wikimedia.org/wiki/File:Earthrise_-_Apollo_8_(39292646471).png.

Crane, M. T. (2014) *Losing Touch with Nature: Literature and the New Science in Sixteenth-century England*. Baltimore: Johns Hopkins University Press.

Crane, S. (2017) 'The Lytel Erthe That Here Is': Environmental Thought in Chaucer's *Parliament of Fowls*. *Studies in the Age of Chaucer: The Yearbook of the New Chaucer Society*, (39), 1–30.

Crane, G. (ed.) (2023) The Perseus Digital Library, 4.0. www.perseus.tufts.edu/hopper/.

Dadabhoy, A. & Mehdizadeh, N. (2023) *Anti-Racist Shakespeare*. Cambridge: Cambridge University Press, Elements in Shakespeare and Pedagogy.

Degenhardt, J. H. (2022) *Globalizing Fortune on the Early Modern Stage*. Oxford: Oxford University Press.

Degenhardt, J. H. & Turner, H. S. (2021) Between Worlds in Shakespeare's Comedy of Errors. *Exemplaria*, 33(2), 158–183.

De Mey, M. (2006) Mastering Ambiguity. In M. Turner (ed.), *The Artful Mind: Cognitive Science and the Riddle of Human Creativity*. New York: Oxford University Press, 271–304.

De Pizan, C. (1997) *The Selected Writings of Christine De Pizan*. Translated by K. Brownlee, Edited by R. Blumenfeld-Kosinski. New York: W.W. Norton.

Desai, A. N. (2019) Topical Shakespeare and the Urgency of Ambiguity. In H. Eklund & W. B. Hyman (eds.), *Teaching Social Justice Through Shakespeare: Why Renaissance Literature Matters Now*. Edinburgh: Edinburgh University Press, 27–35.

Digges, L. & Digges, T. (1576). *A Prognostication Euerlastinge*. London: Thomas Marsh. STC 435.47. Early English Books Online.

Dilek, Y. & Kahya, Ö. (2023). Flood and Earthquake as Punishment of Gods in Antiquity. *Afet Ve Risk Dergisi*, 6(3), 819–828.

Dobson M. (1995) *The Making of the National Poet*. Oxford: Clarendon Press.

Dustagheer, S. & Newman, H. (2018) Metatheatre and Early Modern Drama. *Shakespeare Bulletin*, 36(1), 19–35.

Egan, G. (2010) *The Struggle for Shakespeare's Text*. Cambridge: Cambridge University Press.

Elizabeth I, Queen. (1596) *The Queenes Maiesties Proclamation*. London. STC 8255. Early English Books Online.

Erasmus, D. (1979) *The Praise of Folly*. Translated by & Introduction by C. H. Miller. New Haven: Yale University Press.

Folger Shakespeare Library Digital Collections (2024) https://digitalcollections.folger.edu/.

Froehlich, H. (2019) Moby Dick Is About Whales, or Why Should We Count Words? https://hfroehli.ch/2019/09/27/moby-dick-is-about-whales-or-why-should-we-count-words/.

Gillespie, S. (2016) *Shakespeare's Books: A Dictionary of Shakespeare Sources*. London: Bloomsbury.

Gillies, J. (2016) Globe/Theatrum Mundi. In B. R. Smith, K. Rowe, T. Hoenselaars et al. (eds.), *The Cambridge Guide to the Worlds of Shakespeare*. Cambridge: Cambridge University Press, 60–66.

Goldberg, J. with Frank, M. & Newman, K. (2016) Introduction: World Enough and Time. In M. Frank, K. Newman & J. Goldberg (eds.), *This Distracted Globe: Worldmaking in Early Modern Literature*. New York: Fordham University Press, 9–18.

Green, H. & Green, J. (2012) Crash Course. PBS Digital Studios. www.pbs.org/show/crash-course/.

Greene, R. (2020) *Five Words: Critical Semantics in the Age of Shakespeare and Cervantes*. Chicago: University of Chicago Press.

Griffiths, H. (2021) 'Witchcraft of His Wit': Teaching Shakespeare Through Metaphor. *Metaphor*, 2, 11–14.

Hall, Kim F. (1996) *Things of Darkness: Economies of Race and Gender in Early Modern England*. Ithaca: Cornell University Press.

Hall, E. (2025) *Hall's Chronicles*. Edited by J. D. Mardock. New Internet Shakespeare Editions / Linked Early Modern Drama Online. Victoria: University of Victoria. https://lemdo.uvic.ca/peer-review/emdH5_Hall.html.

Hansen, C. (2017) *Shakespeare and Complexity Theory*. Oxford: Routledge.

Harper, D. (2023) *Online Etymology Dictionary*. www.etymonline.com/.

Holbein the Younger, H. *The Ambassadors*. 1533. Oil on oak, 207 x 209.5 cm. NG1314. London: The National Gallery. https://www.nationalgallery.org.uk/paintings/hans-holbein-the-younger-the-ambassadors.

Holinshed, R. (2025) *Chronicles of England, Scotland, and Ireland*. Edited by J. D. Mardock. New Internet Shakespeare Editions / Linked Early Modern Drama Online. Victoria: University of Victoria. https://lemdo.uvic.ca/peer-review/emdH5_Holinshed.html.

Hollis, G. (2022) Trifling with Catastrophe in *King Lear*. *Studies in English Literature 1500–1900*, 62(1), 245–269.

Honan, P. (1999) *Shakespeare: A Life*. Oxford: Clarendon Press.

Hope, J. (2019) Digital Approaches to Shakespeare's Language. In L. Magnusson & D. Schalkwyk (eds.), *The Cambridge Companion to Shakespeare's Language*. Cambridge: Cambridge University Press, 151–167.

Horowitz, M. C. (2021) Introduction (1): Rival Interpretations of Continent Personification. In Horowitz, M. C. & Arizzoli, L. (eds.), *Bodies and Maps: Early Modern Personifications of The Continents*. Boston: Brill, 1–24.

Houston, D. (2017) Five Maps that Will Change How You See the World. *The Conversation*, https://theconversation.com/five-maps-that-will-change-how-you-see-the-world-74967.

Hyman, W. B. (2022) 'Beyond Beyond': Cymbeline, the Camera Obscura, and the Ontology of Elsewhere. *English Literary Renaissance*, 52(3), 397–412.

Jacobson, T. E. & Mackey, T. P. (2013) Proposing a Metaliteracy Model to Redefine Information Literacy. *Communications in Information Literacy*, 7(2), 84–91.

Jenstad, J., dir. (2006) *The Map of Early Modern London*. Victoria, BC: University of Victoria, 2006–present. https://mapoflondon.uvic.ca.

Jenstad, J. (2022) The Agas Map. In J. Jenstad (ed.), *The Map of Early Modern London*, 7.0. Victoria: University of Victoria. https://mapoflondon.uvic.ca/editions/7.0/map.htm.

Jeromski, A. (2021) MoEML Tutorials. *The Kit Marlowe Project*, https://kitmarlowe.org/moeml-tutorials-2/6774/.

John of S. (1972) *Frivolities of Courtiers and Footprints of Philosophers*. Translated by J. B. Pike. New York: Octagon Books by special arrangement with The University of Minnesota Press.

John of S. (1990) *John of Salisbury: Policraticus*. Edited by C. J. Nederman. Cambridge Texts in the History of Political Thought. Cambridge: Cambridge University Press.

John of S. (1938) *Frivolities of Courtiers and Footprints of Philosophers: Being a Translation of the First, Second, and Third Books and Selections from the Seventh and Eighth Books of the Policraticus*. Translated by J. B. Pike. Minneapolis: University of Minnesota Press.

Kantorowicz, E. (1957) *The King's Two Bodies: A Study in Mediaeval Political Theology*. Princeton: Princeton University Press.

Kennedy, J. M., Kennedy, R., May, S., et al. (eds) (2025) *A Midsummer Night's Dream. A New Variorum Edition of Shakespeare*. Texas: A&M University. https://newvariorumshakespeare.org/edition/mnd/.

Kermode, F. (2000) *Shakespeare's Language*. New York: Farrar, Straus, Giroux.

Kern Paster, G. (2004) *Humouring the Body: Emotions and the Shakespearean Stage*. Chicago: Chicago University Press.

Kline, A. S. (2020) *Ovid's Metamorphoses, tr. Anthony S. Kline: A Complete English Translation and Mythological Index*. https://ovid.lib.virginia.edu/trans/Ovhome.htm.

Lanier, D. M. (2019) *The Merchant of Venice: Language & Writing*. London: The Arden Shakespeare, Arden Student Skills.

Lemon, R. (2012) Law. In A. F. Kinney (ed.), *The Oxford Handbook of Shakespeare*. Oxford: Oxford University Press, 554–570.

Lesser, Z. (2015) *Hamlet After Q1: An Uncanny History of the Shakespearean Text*. Philadelphia: University of Pennsylvania Press.

Lewis, S. L. & Maslin, M. A. (2015) Defining the Anthropocene. *Nature*, 519(7542), 171–180.

Little Jr., A. L. (2023) *White People in Shakespeare*. New York: Bloomsbury.

Lyly, J. (2025) *Euphues and His England*. Edited by J. D. Mardock. New Internet Shakespeare Editions / Linked Early Modern Drama Online. Victoria: University of Victoria. https://lemdo.uvic.ca/peer-review/emdH5_Euphues.html.

Lyne, R. (2011) *Shakespeare, Rhetoric and Cognition*. Cambridge: Cambridge University Press.

Mackey T. P. & Jacobson T. E. (2011) Reframing Information Literacy as Metaliteracy. *College and Research Libraries*, 72(1), 62–78.

Mackey, T. P. & Jacobson, T. E. (2019) *Metaliterate Learning for the Post-Truth World*. Chicago: American Library Association.

MacInnes, I. (2023) English Calendar. http://www.aulis.org/EnglishCalendar/.

Marantz Cohen, P. (2021) *Of Human Kindness: What Shakespeare Teaches Us About Human Empathy*. New Haven: Yale University Press.

McCabe R. A. (1981) Elizabethan Satire and the Bishops' Ban of 1599. *The Yearbook of English Studies*, 11, 188–193.

Mehl, D. (1965) Forms and Functions of the Play within a Play. *Renaissance Drama*, 8, 41–61.

Mentz, S. (2019) *Break Up the Anthropocene*. Minneapolis: University of Minnesota Press.

Merriam-Webster (2023) The Origin of *Hypocrite*: The common word has a dramatic origin story. www.merriam-webster.com/wordplay/hypocrite-meaning-origin.

Moore, P. (1564) *The Hope of Health wherin is conteined a goodlie regimente of life: As medicine, good diet and the goodlie vertues of sonderie herbes, doen by Philip Moore*. London: John Kingston, STC 18069.5. Early English Books Online.

Moreau, E. (2020) Complexion, Temperament and Four Humour Theory in the Renaissance. In M. Sgarbi (ed.), *Encyclopedia of Renaissance Philosophy*. New York: Springer International, 1–3.

Morse, R. (2019) Figures of Speech at Work. In L. Magnusson & D. Schalkwyk (eds.), *The Cambridge Companion to Shakespeare's Language*. Cambridge: Cambridge University Press, 93–114.

Moseley, D., Baumfield, V., Elliot, J. et al. (2005) *Frameworks for Thinking a Handbook for Teaching and Learning*. Cambridge: Cambridge University Press.

Mythopedia (2022) Wasai, LLC. https://mythopedia.com/.

NASA (National Aeronautics and Space Administration) (2017) Chandra Reveals the Elementary Nature of Cassiopeia A. https://chandra.harvard.edu/blog/node/665.

NASA (National Aeronautics and Space Administration) (2019) 2019: Year of the Periodic Table. https://chandra.harvard.edu/chemistry/.

Nashe, T. (1966) *The Works of Thomas Nashe*. Edited by R. B. McKerrow & F. P. Wilson. Vol. 1. Oxford: Basil Blackwell.

Natanson, H., Tierney, L. & Morse, C. E. (2024) Which States Are Restricting, or Requiring, Lessons on Race, Sex and Gender. *The Washington Post*, 4 April. www.washingtonpost.com/education/2024/education-laws-states-teaching-race-gender-sex/.

Nicholl, C. (1994) *The Reckoning: The Murder of Christopher Marlowe*. New York: Harcourt Brace.

Open Source Shakespeare (2023) George Mason University, www.opensourceshakespeare.org/.

Ortelius, A. (1601) *An epitome of Ortelius His Theater of the world*. Antwerp: H. Swingenii for John Norton, STC 18857. Early English Books Online.

Ortelius, A. (1606) *Theatrum Orbis Terrarum*. London: John Norton. Harvard Map Collection, GEN, MO 1.1606 pf*.

Ovid, N. P. (2023) *The Metamorphoses*. Translated by A. S. Kline, Charlottesville: University of Virginia Libraries, https://ovid.lib.virginia.edu/trans/Ovhome.htm#askline. Oxford English Dictionary, Oxford University Press, July 2023.

Palingenio Stellato, M. (1588) *The zodiake of life*. Translated by B. Googe. London: Robert Robinson. STC 19152. Early English Books Online.

Paris, J. (2021) Bad Blood, Black Desires: On the Fragility of Whiteness in Middleton and Rowley's *The Changeling*. *Early Theatre*, 24(1), 113–137.

Peele, G. (1593) *The honour of the garter*. London, STC 19539, *EEBO*, www.proquest.com/books/honour-garter-displaied-poeme-gratulatorie/docview/2240901415/se-2 (accessed April 26, 2025).

Petronius, G. (1922) *The Satyricon, Vol. 3 (Encolpius and His Companions)*. Translated by W. C. Firebaugh. (rpt. 2004) Project Gutenberg, www.gutenberg.org/files/5220/5220-h/5220-h.htm.

Phillips, L. (2021) The Medical Astrologer's Toolkit: Part I. In *Medical Astrology: Science, Art, and Influence in Early-Modern Europe*, Yale University Library Online Exhibitions. https://onlineexhibits.library.yale.edu/s/medicalastrology/page/the-medical-astrologer-s-toolkit-part-ii.

Phillips, L. (2023) *Medical Astrology: Science, Art, and Influence in Early Modern Europe*. Yale University Library, https://onlineexhibits.library.yale.edu/s/medicalastrology/page/introduction.

Plato. (1988) *The Laws of Plato*. Translated by T. L. Pangle. Chicago: University of Chicago Press.

Plutarch. (1957) *Moralia*. Translated by H. F. Cherniss & W. C. Helmbold. Cambridge, MA: Harvard University Press, Loeb Classical Library, XII.

Pumphrey, S. (2011) 'Your Astronomers and Ours Differ Exceedingly': The Controversy over the 'New Star' of 1572 in the Light of a Newly Discovered Text by Thomas Digges. *BJHS* 44(1), 29–60.

Purcell, S. (2018) Are Shakespeare's Plays Always Metatheatrical? *Shakespeare Bulletin*, 36(1), 19–35.

Pye, V. C. (2017) *Unearthing Shakespeare: Embodied Performance and the Globe*. Oxford: Routledge.

Raleigh, W. (1614) *The History of the World*. London: W. Burre. STC 20640. Internet Archive, https://archive.org/details/historyofworld00rale/page/n9/mode/2up.

Ramachandran, A. (2015) *The Worldmakers: Global Imagining in Early Modern Europe*. Chicago: University of Chicago Press.

Richards, J. (2019) *Voices and Books in the English Renaissance: A New History of Reading*. Oxford: Oxford University Press.

Roberts, J. P. (2018) Conceptual Blending, the Second Naïveté, and the Emergence of New Meanings. *Open Theology*, 4(1), 29–45.

Rollo-Koster, J. (2017) Body Politic. *Encyclopedia Britannica*. www.britannica.com/topic/body-politic.

Rowling, J. K. (2007) *Harry Potter and the Deathly Hallows*. New York: Scholastic Books.

Roychoudhury, S. (2018) *Phantasmic Shakespeare: Imagination in the Age of Early Modern Science*. Ithaca: Cornell University Press.

Ruge, E. (2014) Having a Good Time at the Theatre of the World: Amusement, Anthitheatricality, and the Calvinist Use of the *Theatrum Mundi* Metaphor in Early Modern England. In B. Quiring (ed.), *If Then the World a Theatre Present: Revisions of the Theatrum Mundi Metaphor in Early Modern England*. Boston: De Gruyter, 25–38.

Rutter, T. (2024) *Shakespeare & Science*. Oxford: Oxford University Press.

Sarkar, D. (2019) Literary Justice: The Participatory Ethics of Early Modern Possible Words. In H. Eklund & W. B. Hyman (eds.), *Teaching Social Justice Through Shakespeare: Why Renaissance Literature Matters Now*. Edinburgh: Edinburgh University Press, 174–186.

Sarkar, D. (2023) *Possible Knowledge: The Literary Forms of Early Modern Science*. Philadelphia: University of Pennsylvania Press.

Sarkar, D. (2024) Naturalizing Race and Racialised Geographies. In P. Akhime (ed.), *The Oxford Handbook of Shakespeare and Race*. Oxford: Oxford University Press, 52–70.

Scott, J. C. (2017) *Against the Grain: A Deep History of the Earliest States*. New Haven: Yale University Press.

Scovell, G. (2023) Which Supernova Did Tycho Observe in 1572? *Astronomy*. www.astronomy.com/science/which-supernova-did-tycho-observe-in-1572/.

Semler, L. E. (2013) *Teaching Shakespeare and Marlowe Learning Versus the System*. London: Bloomsbury.

Semler, L. E. (2016) Prosperous Teaching and the Thing of Darkness: Raising a *Tempest* in the classroom. *Cogent Arts & Humanities*, 3(1), 1–10.

Seneca, L. A. (1999) *Natural Questions*. Translated by T. H. Corcoran. Cambridge, MA: Harvard University Press, Loeb Classical Library.

Shakeserendipity. (2015) *Shakespeare Reloaded*. https://shakespearereloaded.edu.au/activities/shakeserendipity.

Shakespeare, W. (1600) The Most Excellent Historie of the Merchant of Venice. *Shakespeare Documented*, https://shakespearedocumented.folger.edu/resource/document/merchant-venice-first-edition.

Shakespeare, W. (1603) *The Tragicall Historie of Hamlet Prince of Denmarke by William Shake-Speare*. London: [V. Simmes] for N. [Ling] & I. [J.] Trundell. STC 22275. Early English Books Online.

Shakespeare, W. (1604) *The Tragicall Historie of Hamlet, Prince of Denmarke*. London: I [J.] R[oberts] for N. L[ing]. STC 222276. Early English Books Online.

Shakespeare, W. (1623) *Mr. William Shakespeares Comedies, Histories, & Tragedies: Published according to the True Originall Copies*. Edited by J. Heminge & H. Condell. London: Printed by I. Jaggard and E. Blount.

STC 22273. Fo. 1, No. 68, https://digitalcollections.folger.edu/bib78903-80936.

Shakespeare, W. (2006a) *Hamlet*. Edited by A. Thompson & N. Taylor. The Arden Shakespeare, Third Series. London: Bloomsbury.

Shakespeare, W. (2006b) *The Merchant of Venice*. Edited by L. S. Marcus. New York: Norton Critical Editions.

Shakespeare, W. (2007a) *Hamlet: The Texts of 1603 and 1623*. Edited by A. Thompson & N. Taylor. London: The Arden Shakespeare.

Shakespeare, W. (2007b) *Othello*. Edited by K. F. Hall. Boston: Bedford St. Martin's.

Shakespeare, W. (2009) *Love's Labour's Lost*. Edited by W. C. Carroll. Cambridge: New Cambridge Shakespeare.

Shakespeare, W. (2010) *The Merchant of Venice*. Edited by J. Drakakis. London: The Arden Shakespeare, Third Series.

Shakespeare, W. (2024a) *A Midsummer Night's Dream*. Edited by B. Mowat, P. Werstine, M. Poston & R. Niles. Washington, DC: Folger Shakespeare Library. www.folger.edu/explore/shakespeares-works/a-midsummer-nights-dream/read.

Shakespeare, W. (2024b) *As You Like It*. Edited by B. Mowat, P. Werstine, M. Poston & R. Niles. Washington, DC: Folger Shakespeare Library. www.folger.edu/explore/shakespeares-works/as-you-like-it/read/.

Shakespeare, W. (2024c) *Hamlet*. Edited by D. Bevington. Internet Shakespeare Editions. Victoria: University of Victoria. https://internetshakespeare.uvic.ca/Library/Texts/Ham/index.html#toc_Introduction.

Shakespeare, W. (2024d) Hamlet (Quarto 1, 1603). In D. Bevington (ed.), *Hamlet*. Internet Shakespeare Editions. Victoria: University of Victoria. https://internetshakespeare.uvic.ca/doc/Ham_Q1/index.html.

Shakespeare, W. (2024e) Hamlet (Quarto 2, 1604). In D. Bevington (ed.), *Hamlet*. Internet Shakespeare Editions. Victoria: University of Victoria. https://internetshakespeare.uvic.ca/doc/Ham_Q2/index.html.

Shakespeare, W. (2024f) Hamlet (Folio 1, 1623). In D. Bevington (ed.), *Hamlet*. Internet Shakespeare Editions. Victoria: University of Victoria. https://internetshakespeare.uvic.ca/doc/Ham_F1/.

Shakespeare, W. (2024g) *Henry V*. Edited by B. Mowat, P. Werstine, M. Poston & R. Niles. Washington, DC: Folger Shakespeare Library, n.d. www.folger.edu/explore/shakespeares-works/henry-v/read/.

Shakespeare, W. (2024h) *Shakespeare's Plays, Sonnets and Poems*. Edited by B. Mowat, P. Werstine, M. Poston & R. Niles. Washington, DC: Folger Shakespeare Library, n.d. https://folger.edu/explore/shakespeares-works/all-works.

Shakespeare, W. (2024i) The Folger Shakespeare API Tools. Encoded by M. Poston. www.folgerdigitaltexts.org/api.

Shakespeare, W. (2025) *Henry V*. Edited by J. D. Mardock. New Internet Shakespeare Editions / Linked Early Modern Drama Online. Victoria: University of Victoria. https://lemdo.uvic.ca/peer-review/emdH5_edition.html.

Shakespeare Documented (2024) Stationers' Register entry for *As You Like it, Henry V*, and *Much Ado About Nothing* 'to be staied.' https://shakespearedocumented.folger.edu/resource/document/stationers-register-entry-you-it-henry-v-and-much-ado-about-nothing-be-staied.

Shakespeare Redrawn (2020) *Shakespeare Reloaded*. www.shakespearereloaded.edu.au/events/shakespeare-redrawn.

Shapiro, J. (2005) *1599: A Year in the Life of William Shakespeare*. New York: Harper Collins.

Shapiro, J. (2006) *1599: A Year in the Life of William Shakespeare*. London: Faber and Faber.

Singh, V. (2024) *Teaching Climate Change: Science, Stories, Justice*. London: Routledge.

Smith, E. (2019) *This Is Shakespeare: How to Read the World's Greatest Playwright*. London: Pelican Books.

Smith, E. (2021) *This Is Shakespeare*. New York: Vintage Books.

Smith, I. (2022) *Black Shakespeare: Reading and Misreading Race*. Cambridge: Cambridge University Press.

Smith, E. (rpt. 2023) *Shakespeare's First Folio: Four Centuries of an Iconic Book*. Oxford: Oxford University Press.

Sobolev, D. (2008) Metaphor Revisited. *New Literary History*, 39(4), 903–929.

Speed, J. (1631) *A Prospect of the Most Famous Parts of the World*. London: I [J.] Dawson for G. Humble. STC 23040. https://digitalcollections.folger.edu/bib169384-164710.

Spenser, E. (1978) *The Faerie Queene*. Translated by T. P. Roche with C. P. O'Donnell, Jr. New York: Penguin Books.

Steffen, W. H. (2023) *Anthropocene Theater and the Shakespearean Stage*. Oxford: Oxford University Press.

Steggle, M. (2018) The Humours in Humour: Shakespeare and Early Modern Psychology. In H. Hirschfeld (ed.), *The Oxford Handbook of Shakespearean Comedy*. Oxford: Oxford University Press, 220–235.

Stern, T. (2013) 'This Wide and Universal Theatre': The Theatre as Prop in Shakespeare's Metadrama. In F. Karim-Cooper & T. Stern (eds.), *Shakespeare's Theatres and the Effects of Performance*. London: Bloomsbury, 11–32.

Stern, J. A., Barbarin, O., & Cassidy, J. (2021) Working Toward Anti-Racist Perspectives in Attachment Theory, Research, and Practice. *Attachment & Human Development*, 1–31.doi: 10.1080/14616734.2021.1976933.

Tesich, S. (1992) A government of lies. *The Free Library*. www.thefreelibrary.com/Agovernmentoflies.-a011665982.

Thompson, A. & Turchi, L. (2016) *Teaching Shakespeare with Purpose: A Student-Centred Approach*. London: Bloomsbury Arden Shakespeare.

Tillyard, E. M. W. (1959) *The Elizabethan World Picture*. New York: Vintage Books.

Traub, V. (ed.) (2016) *The Oxford Handbook of Shakespeare and Embodiment: Gender, Sexuality, and Race*. Oxford: Oxford University Press.

Waldron, J. (2022) The Politics of Scale in Shakespeare's *Henry V*: Fiction, History, Theater. *English Literary Renaissance*, 52(3), 439–451. www.journals.uchicago.edu/doi/abs/10.1086/721067.

Watkins, J. (1792) An Essay Toward a History of Bideford, in the County of Devon. Exeter: E. Grigg. www.google.com/books/edition/An_Essay_Towards_a_History_of_Bideford_i/iW9bAAAAQAAJ?hl=en.

Watson, R. N. (2014) Shakespeare's Coining of Words. In M. Saenger & J. Loehlin (eds.), *Interlinguicity, Internationality and Shakespeare*. Montreal: McGill-Queen's University Press, 86–106.

Weiland, T. (2022) The Science of Data, Data Science: Perversions and Possibilities in the Anthropocene Through a Spatial Justice Lens. In M. F. J. Wallace, J. Bazzul, M. Higgins & S. Tolbert (eds.), *Reimagining Science Education in the Anthropocene*. Cham: Palgrave Macmillan, Palgrave Studies in Education and the Environment, 183–199.

Wells, S. & Taylor, G. with Jowett, J. & Montgomery, W. (rpt. 1997) *William Shakespeare: A Textual Companion*. Oxford: Oxford University Press.

Wick, J. (2004) Parallax Example. JustinWick at English Wikipedia, CC BY-SA 3.0, http://creativecommons.org/licenses/by-sa/3.0/.

Woods, G. with Seymour, L. (2019) Learning and Teaching Resources. In K. Britland & L. Cottegnies (eds.), *King Henry V: A Critical Reader*. London: The Arden Shakespeare, 221–246.

Wright, G.T. (1981) Hendiadys and Hamlet. *PMLA*. March, 168–193.

Yates, F. A. (1936) *A Study of Love's Labour's Lost*. Cambridge: Cambridge University Press.

Žižek, S. (2006) *The Parallax View*. Cambridge, MA: The MIT Press.

Acknowledgements

To my students, colleagues, mentors and friends who generously answered cries for help and supported me in so many ways throughout this project, I invoke inexpressible gratitude: Elaine Beilin, Joseph Campana, Bill Carroll, Olivia Copeland, Gerry Cox, Mary Crane, Jane Hwang Degenhardt, Craig Dionne, Lisa Eck, Andy Fleck, Liz Fox, Jeffrey Goodhind, David Grophear, Claire Hansen, Diana Henderson, Jonathan Hope, Janelle Jenstad, Coppélia Kahn, Scott Maisano, Steve Mentz, David Morrow, Mary MacDonald, Desmond McCarthy, Linda McJannet, Thomas Norris, Sim Ong, Jamie Paris, Anita Raychawdhuri, Austin Rifflemacher, Jennifer Richards, Marjorie Rubright, Liam Semler, Emma Smith, Ilana Talamo, Henry Turner, Andrea Walkden, Grayson Welch and Owen Williams. I wish this list were complete – please forgive my omissions.

This project also benefitted much from time spent as a Visiting Scholar at the Arthur F. Kinney Center for Interdisciplinary Renaissance Studies, and from sharing work in progress at the Folger Research Colloquium: 'World, Globe Planet: The Scales of Relation in Early Modernity', at the Shakespearean Studies seminar at Harvard and at the Shakespeare Association of America.

To Jason and our menagerie of research assistants, thank you for being lovely and funny throughout. I'd love to attribute any mistakes here to one of the cats, but they're surely my own.

I dedicate this project to the memory of my cousin Tim Orrok. Tim, part of the team that first landed humans on the moon, generously shared with me his love of both the stars and Shakespeare.

Cambridge Elements

Shakespeare and Pedagogy

Liam E. Semler

The University of Sydney

Liam E. Semler is Professor of Early Modern Literature in the Department of English at the University of Sydney. He is author of Teaching Shakespeare and Marlowe: Learning versus the System (2013) and co-editor (with Kate Flaherty and Penny Gay) of Teaching Shakespeare beyond the Centre: Australasian Perspectives (2013). He is editor of Coriolanus: A Critical Reader (2021) and co-editor (with Claire Hansen and Jackie Manuel) of Reimagining Shakespeare Education: Teaching and Learning through Collaboration (Cambridge, forthcoming). His most recent book outside Shakespeare studies is The Early Modern Grotesque: English Sources and Documents 1500–1700 (2019). Liam leads the Better Strangers project which hosts the open-access Shakespeare Reloaded website (shakespearereloaded.edu.au).

Gillian Woods

University of Oxford

Gillian Woods is an Associate Professor and Tutorial Fellow in English at Magdalen College, University of Oxford. She is the author of *Shakespeare's Unreformed Fictions* (2013; joint winner of Shakespeare's Globe Book Award), *Romeo and Juliet: A Reader's Guide to Essential Criticism* (2012), and numerous articles about Renaissance drama. She is the co-editor (with Sarah Dustagheer) of *Stage Directions and Shakespearean Theatre* (2018). She is currently working on a new edition of

A *Midsummer Night's Dream* for Cambridge University Press, as well as a Leverhulme-funded monograph about Renaissance Theatricalities. As founding director of the Shakespeare Teachers' Conversations, she runs a seminar series that brings together university academics, school teachers and educationalists from non-traditional sectors, and she regularly runs workshops for schools.

ADVISORY BOARD

Janelle Jenstad, *University of Victoria*

Farah Karim-Cooper, *Shakespeare's Globe*

Bi-qi Beatrice Lei, *National Taiwan University*

Florence March, *Université Paul-Valéry Montpellier*

Peggy O'Brien, *Folger Shakespeare Library*

Paul Prescott, *University of California Merced*

Abigail Rokison-Woodall, *University of Birmingham*

Emma Smith, *University of Oxford*

Patrick Spottiswoode, *Shakespeare's Globe*

Jenny Stevens, *English Association*

Ayanna Thompson, *Arizona State University*

Joe Winston, *University of Warwick*

About the Series
The teaching and learning of Shakespeare around the world is complex and changing. Elements in Shakespeare and Pedagogy synthesises theory and practice, including provocative, original pieces of research, as well as dynamic, practical engagements with learning contexts.

Cambridge Elements

Shakespeare and Pedagogy

Elements in the Series

Podcasts and Feminist Shakespeare Pedagogy
Varsha Panjwani

Anti-Racist Shakespeare
Ambereen Dadabhoy and Nedda Mehdizadeh

Teaching Shakespeare and His Sisters: An Embodied Approach
Emma Whipday

Shakespeare and Place-Based Learning
Claire Hansen

Critical Pedagogy and Active Approaches to Teaching Shakespeare
Jennifer Kitchen

Teaching with Interactive Shakespeare Editions
Laura B. Turchi

Disavowing Authority in the Shakespeare Classroom
Huw Griffiths

The Pedagogy of Watching Shakespeare
Bethan Marshall, Myfanwy Edwards and Charlotte Dixie

Teaching English as a Second Language with Shakespeare
Fabio Ciambella

Shakespeare and Neurodiversity
Laura Seymour

Transdisciplinary Shakespeare Pedagogy
Coen Heijes

Teaching Shakespeare's Theatre of the World
Kristen Abbott Bennett

A full series listing is available at: www.cambridge.org/ESPG

For EU product safety concerns, contact us at Calle de José Abascal, 56–1°,
28003 Madrid, Spain or eugpsr@cambridge.org.

www.ingramcontent.com/pod-product-compliance
Lightning Source LLC
LaVergne TN
LVHW011844060526
838200LV00054B/4164